Publish Your First Book

A Quick Start Guide to

Professional Publishing in the Digital Age

Karl W. Palachuk

Published by

Great Little Book Publishing

Sacramento, CA

www.GreatLittleBook.com

www.PublishYourFirstBook.com

Great Little Book Publishing
2121 Natomas Crossing Dr., #200
Sacramento, CA 95834

Publish Your First Book: A Quick Start Guide to Professional Publishing in the Digital Age

Copyright © 2011 by Karl W. Palachuk

All rights reserved.

Printed in the United States of America.

No part of this book may be used or reproduced in any manner whatsoever without written permission.

www.greatlittlebook.com

ISBN: 978-0-9819978-4-1

Library of Congress Control Number: 2011928545

Publish Your First Book

A Quick Start Guide to Professional Publishing in the Digital Age

Karl W. Palachuk

Table of Contents

Section I: Getting Started 13

Chapter 1 – This Guide 13

Chapter 2 – About the Author 17

Chapter 3 – Writing Non-Fiction 21

Chapter 4 – Process Overview 27

Chapter 5 – Begin with the End In Mind 35

Chapter 6 – Your Marketing Plan 41

Chapter 7 – Budget and Cash Flow Projection 49

Section II: Resources..53

www.PublishYourFirstBook.com

Chapter 8 – Interns and Other "Staff" 53

Chapter 9 – Local Writers / Publishers / Editors 57

Chapter 10 – Outsourcing on the Internet 61

Section III: Some Mechanics and Technical Stuff 69

Chapter 11 – Legal and Tax Issues 69

Chapter 12 – ISBNs 75

Chapter 13 – Some Design Considerations 85

Chapter 14 – Library of Congress 93

Chapter 15 – Copyrights 101

Section IV: Editing, Layout, and Production 107

Chapter 16 – Layout 107

Chapter 17 – Copy Editing 115

Chapter 18 – Cover Design 121

Chapter 19 – Cover Template and Production Variables 127

Chapter 20 – Uploading PDFs 135

Chapter 21 – Drafts and Review Copies 139

Section V: Printing and Distribution 143

Chapter 22 – Lightning Source / Ingram Books 143

Chapter 23 – Lulu, Amazon, and Other Alternatives 147

Chapter 24 – Kindle and Other "Readers" 155

Chapter 25 – Self-Distribution 163

Section VI: Integrating Your Web Site, Mailing List, and Payment Systems 169

Chapter 26 – First Step: A Mailing List 169

Chapter 27 – Be Ready to Take Money 175

Chapter 28 – Store Software 185

Chapter 29 – Building Your Web Site 191

Chapter 30 – Bundling 197

Chapter 31 – Your Other Services 201

Section VII: Sales, Marketing, and Promotion 205

Chapter 32 – Pricing for Non-Fiction 205

Chapter 33 – Your Marketing Plan (Revised) 215

Chapter 34 – Using Social Media Effectively 223

Chapter 35 – Give-Aways and Samples 229

Chapter 36 – When Promotion Becomes Product 233

Chapter 37 – Gimmicks, Gotchas, and Schemes to Avoid 239

Section VIII: Final Analysis 245

Chapter 38 – Congratulations 245

Chapter 39 – Launch Party? 247

Chapter 40 – How Would You Do This Again? 257

Resources 261

Connect With Me Online 269

Dedication

This book is dedicated to two people who have had a great influence on my publishing "career" over the years.

Harry Brelsford from SMB Nation embraced my first book with enthusiasm. Harry's support and assistance made that book a true jumping-off place for my publishing career.

Harry has been a friend, business partner, and mentor for many years and I am grateful for everything he has done for me and for the communities he serves.

Stephanie Chandler of Authority Publishing has likewise been my friend, mastermind partner, and mentor. Her excitement over this business and her dedication to making writing and publishing a central part of her success has taught me a great deal.

So I dedicate this book to these two great mentors in my life. They might not agree with the contents of this book or my specific approach to publishing. So please hold me responsible for the contents herein and recognize them as great influences in my personal and professional lives.

    -- Karl W. Palachuk

About the Author

Karl W. Palachuk is a business owner, entrepreneur, speaker, author, and Small Business Consultant. He has owned several successful businesses, primarily in the fields of technical consulting and book publishing. As a trainer and coach Karl has worked with thousands of business owners and managers to help them create and implement successful business models.

This is Karl's ninth book. All of his books are non-fiction and most were written for computer consultants. One exception is *Relax Focus Succeed: A Guide To Balancing Your Personal And Professional Lives And Being More Successful In Both*. Relax Focus Succeed® is Karl's framework for balancing your life and finding success in all areas of your life (work, home, romance, parenthood, etc.).

Karl has been a featured speaker at conferences and seminars over the last fifteen years. He is a Microsoft Certified Systems Engineer with a Bachelor's Degree from Gonzaga University and a Master's Degree from The University of Michigan. He is also a Microsoft Small Business Specialist, and has been on advisory panels for a variety of companies and professional organizations.

www.PublishYourFirstBook.com

Acknowledgements

After writing many books, and being involved in the process over many years, I have settled into a process that works very well for me. And that process requires a team of experts.

Svetlana Shurayev deserves first mention as this is now the fourth book she's been involved in on the technical side. Every day Lana makes my business more successful with her dedication to customer service and excellence.

On the rare occasion with a new book is in the works, she shines even brighter, taking on the role of project manager and making sure all the pieces come together as they should.

My other "production" staff include Chris Sandoval, and John Wicks. These folks all have regular jobs at Great Little Book but jump in to take on whatever project I come up with on a given day.

Chris is our graphics designer and one of our web developers. He makes sure the web sites look good and we have handsome logos for all of our online and printed marketing.

John is our principle web developer and manages our online presence, which includes hundreds of different web sites. For this project John did a huge amount of work to prepare the related web sites and "landing pages" for the book launch.

Monica Caraway runs our office, manages all my appearances, and assists with all the promotion and marketing for the various brands we have at Great Little Book. Jerry Kennedy is our "Opportunity Architect," which translates into some kind of sales management. He sells me to larger companies and keeps the lights on for us.

Great Little Book is a great place to work because of the willingness of a great bunch of people to come together every day, have fun, and see what kind of mischief we can get into. It's a formula that works.

Finally, I thank Ronda Snyder for being my creative inspiration. As a technical consultant I tend to spend a lot of time with the left side of my brain. As a painter and all around artist, Ronda inspires me to explore everything more deeply. This book was written in a fit of creativity that she inspired. And for that I am grateful.

    -- Karl W. Palachuk

Section I: Getting Started

Chapter 1 – This Guide

As a published author in two different fields, I am often asked about the topics of my books. Whether you've already written your book or you are about to write it, you can look forward to positioning yourself as an "expert" in your field – simply because you've published a book!

But, in addition to my subject matter knowledge, I am often asked about my book publishing experience. After all, it is a specialized knowledge.

So sometimes, as I travel around, I am asked by authors (and prospective authors) how to go about publishing a book. At that point I find myself giving a "brain dump" on my publishing experience. This ranges from choosing a topic to printing, publishing, distribution, and even endorsements.

Most new authors have a handful of common questions. But I give them my brain dump on a whole lot more – because new authors don't know what they don't know. They don't know about ISBN numbers or digital printing. Or they have assumptions and misconceptions about how the publishing world works.

After many of these conversations, I realized that I was dishing out the same information again and again. And, over time, I actually began to dish it out in an organized manner. After one of these discussions I decided to formalize my brain dump and put it in writing.

There are lots of books . . . LOTS of books . . . on the topics of writing and publishing. There are whole books written on each of the topics in this little guide. My goal is not to replace those books, but to give a "quick and dirty" guide of just the things you really need to know when you get started as a new author or publisher.

Throughout this book, and consolidated at the end, I have provided some additional resources. So when it's time to dig a little deeper, I hope you'll find a few places to get started.

Please note that I am a very opinionated person. So I'm not going to try to paint a "fair" picture about anything. This guide lays out what I know and what I believe about the subject of self-publishing.

I have written lots of books, white papers, blogs, and information products. So I *could* make this book much longer if I wanted to. But my goal is to give the first time publisher just the key information needed for a successful first book.

Keep a Journal

As you go through this book, I highly recommend that you keep a journal. Write down ideas. Make lists of things to do. Create checklists for yourself.

Believe it or not, almost every chapter in this book could be expanded to be a book. There are already many books on some of these topics (book design is a major at some colleges). So my job is to give you enough of an introduction to make your first book as professional as possible.

But guess what? Two things will be different at the end of the book publishing process. First, the world of digital publishing will have evolved. This business moves at the speed of light, but you'll need to keep notes on what worked, what didn't work, and what you will do differently next time.

The other thing that will be different at the end of the book is *you*. Now you're an author working to create a quality book. When you're done you'll be a publisher with one book already in the system. You may or may not want to ever do this a second time. But if you do, you'll have your own personal experiences to guide you.

I certainly welcome you feedback on this book. Please email me at karlp@greatlittlebook.com.

Enjoy!

Chapter 2 – About the Author

Even though there's a brief "About the Author" section in the front matter of this book, I thought it would be nice to answer the question of . . .

What makes me eligible to give you advice on writing a book?

I run two businesses in Sacramento, CA. One is a technology consulting company. The other is a book publishing company, which grew out of my activities publishing over a dozen books for myself and others.

I have written eight books prior to this one. I self-published seven of those and worked with another small company that self-published the other one.

My first book was published way back in 2005-2006 when digital printing was neither cheap nor widespread. Back in those dark ages, the only way to get a good price on book printing was to buy 1,000 copies at a time.

My first book cost about eight dollars to produce, when printed in quantities of 1,000 at a time. In other words, I had to come up with $8,000 in order to get a garage full of books to sell. I had to *really* believe that I was going to be able to sell these books in order to commit to that printing!

As you'll see when we discuss pricing, however, I am very happy to be publishing in the non-fiction market. Why? Because I can charge a lot more for my books than I would ever get for a work of fiction.

I didn't need to sell 500 books to get my money back. In fact, that book sold for $90. So even with give-aways and promotions, I had to sell only one hundred books to recoup my investment. And, as you can imagine, I had quite of bit of profit by the time the first 1,000 books were gone.

Because of my publications, I have been able to build my "publishing" career to include speaking at professional conferences, paid trainings for major vendors, and a whole series of add-on and spin-off products. I have also developed an online store that is focused on my core market (technical consultants).

Let me be very clear on this point: It took a great deal of work to build up all of those spin-off products, training materials, web sites, and so forth. It took time and money and hard work.

But let me also assure you that it is very realistic that you can build a little "empire" of your own around your products. It begins with your expertise and knowledge. Then it proceeds to your book, to speaking engagements, to additional work, and on from there.

This book is not intended to give you any assistance on writing, and very little on designing or formatting your book. I have to draw the line somewhere. I can't help you write. And since I recommend that you outsource the layout and design aspects, I cover those by recommending you don't do them yourself.

Whether you intend to write just one book or build an empire, I hope this book helps you to get started.

Chapter 3 – Writing Non-Fiction

There's one very big division in the world of writing: Fiction vs. Non-Fiction. I don't write fiction, so I am not trying to give advice in the world of fiction.

Most of the mechanics of production and distribution are the same for both fiction and non-fiction. But there are some very important differences, primarily around money and profitability. As I mentioned a few pages ago, non-fiction books can be priced much higher than fiction books. This is because non-fiction books are often sold as tools rather than entertainment.

Fiction books sell for very slim margins and need huge distribution and sales in order to bring significant income to the author. Non-fiction books can be priced much higher and are easily combined with training and other professional services. So the payback is faster and profits are higher.

Self Publishing is another important factor. If you go to a big publisher, they're need to sell 10,000 or 20,000 copies *minimum* before they will be interested in your book. If you're lucky, you'll get a small advance. To earn anything beyond that, you'll need to be very lucky!

As a self-publisher, even in the world of fiction, you need much smaller numbers to break even or make a profit. Consider my books. I have several books that sell in the range of $50-$100 each. My cost of production on these is around $6-$10, depending on the size of the book and whether it includes a CD.

So my profit for each book is in the range of $40 to $94 per book. If I can sell 1,000 copies, I've got a nice little return no matter where it falls in that price range. I would have a great deal of difficulty selling 20,000 copies of any one book. But, man, if I do, it will be a great payday for me! So, you see, the economics of self-publishing allow the author to make a lot more money by selling a much smaller quantity.

Non-Fiction has other advantages as well. Near the end of the book I discuss spin-off products. These are all the "other things" you can sell besides books.

The world of non-fiction publishing begins with your expertise. You are writing a book because you have specialized knowledge to pass on to other people. I'm not sure what it is about a book, but any author can tell you: Having a book elevates you into "expert" status even if no one reads the book.

Book and expert status can be leveraged into speaking engagements in your field of expertise. If you decide you want to put the energy into you, you can build a following and a series of products from there.

It's not magic. You have to work hard. But there are much *harder* ways to make a living!

Michael Larsen, literary agent, consultant, author of How to *Write a Book Proposal*

Q: Do you participate in local groups of writers or publishers? Why?

A: Writer's groups are an essential way of building a community of writers, getting feedback on your work, and learning about agents, publishers, and the business. One reason why the San Francisco Bay Area is the best place in the world to be a writer is that it's the second leading publishing center in the country, so there's a wealth of events and organizations for writers. We participate in writing events and organizations as speakers and attendees. We are also creating a community of writers with the San Francisco Writers Conference and the San Francisco Writers University.

Q: Have you used speaking engagements to promote your books? What advice can you offer to new authors and publishers?

A: I speak at writer's groups and conferences that sell my three writing-related books. When you speak, you reach both attendees and their communities, online and off. It's an excellent opportunity to sell books and mention your other prod-

ucts and services. You and your book also benefit from the publicity for the event. Start speaking as soon as you're ready to test-market your book and build your visibility and the audience for your book, and to promote whatever you're doing.

Q: Do you create business plans and marketing plans for your books? Is this really necessary for a first time author?

A: Have a five-year plan for where you want to go and discuss it with successful authors in your field. Also have literary goals and publishing goals for your book: what you want it to be and achieve, and what future you want for it.

Big and midsize publishers expect authors to have a promotion plan, list what they will do to promote their book. Even novelists are submitting a plan. Small houses would like a promotion plan but don't require it. So whether writers should submit one depends on their publishing goals.

Q: What other advice do you have for people who are working to publish their first book?

- Be passionate about your books and communicating with your readers
- Become an expert on the kind of book you're writing
- Set daily work goals
- Be creative in every aspect of your work

- Serve your readers as well as you can
- Have faith in your work and yourself
- Summon the courage you need to meet the challenges you will encounter
- Understand how publishers and agents work, how the business is changing, and how to use technology
- Be devoted to using reading, researching, revising, and sharing your work to ensure it's as well conceived and crafted as you can make it
- Create communities of fans and professionals to help you
- Be a contentpreneur: make your work scalable, make your smartphone and laptop your office; keep turning out work; re-purpose your work in as many forms, media, and countries as possible; be committed and resourceful; learn to collaborate to create new products and services.
- Be patient about developing your work, visibility, and career

Michael Larsen is a literary agent and consultant to nonfiction writers. He and his partner Elizabeth Pomada are co-directors of the San Francisco Writers Conference and the San Francisco Writing for Change Conference.

He is the author of the third editions of How to Write a Book Proposal and How to Get a Literary Agent, and coauthor of the second edition of Guerrilla Marketing for Writers: 100 Weapons for Selling Your Work. Michael blogs at http://sfwriters.info/blog. His literary agency web site is www.larsenpomada.com. The San Francisco Writers University web site is www.sfwritersu.com.

Chapter 4 – Process Overview

When you don't know about a topic, everything seems difficult and complicated. As soon as you master the knowledge and work your way through the process, it becomes a lot easier and less mysterious.

As a "newbie" in the world of publishing, you probably have a lot of questions about the nuts and bolts. We'll get to that, but let's start with an overview.

Again, I won't give you any advice on writing your book *per se*. I have plenty of advice on making it look professional. But the content is something you need to come up with on your own.

I do recommend that you go to the trouble of outlining some kind of business plan and marketing plan for your book. My favorite resource along these lines is *How to Write a Book Proposal* by Michael Larsen.

The process of writing a book proposal (or business plan, or marketing plan) will help you keep your feet planted firmly on the ground. All too often, authors have a vision that they'll write a book and become suddenly wealthy. That *has* happened, but only to about seven people in the history of the world. So don't think you'll be the 8th lucky author.

A business plan will start out blank, but you'll fill it in as you calculate expenses for layout, "proof" copies, marketing, and so forth.

Some writers like to write the whole book without regard to the final formatting or layout. Thoughts about fonts, margins, headers, tables, etc. can be distracting while you're writing. As you gain experience in the way *you* like to write, you can adjust your habits.

I have developed a process of working one chapter at a time. For this book, I'm working one section at a time because the chapters are intended to be very brief. As I finish chapters, I send them off to a rough layout. I figure out what I want the inside of the book to look like.

Once that's in place, I give a template to Lana on my team and she puts the chapters into that template. While she's at it, she reads through the text to see if I missed any spelling, formatting, or other errors.

While she's working on that, I'm working on another chapter. It might not be the next chapter, however. One of the great things about non-fiction is that you can write the chapters in any order. I tend to carry a folder with me for each chapter I'm working on with notes and printouts of relevant information.

I leave the "front matter" chapter open pretty much until I'm finished with the book. I might write the dedication or introduction at any time. But I can't finalize the intro and overview until I'm done with the rest of the book.

So, anyway, I feed chapters to Lana as I finish them and she pieces them together. Slowly, the book takes shape.

As you're working on that, you should begin the process of designing the book cover. As you'll read again when we get to that chapter, this is an area that definitely needs a professional. Your "professional" might be a student intern, an employee, or someone you found on the internet. Whoever it is, begin the work on the cover while the book is being written.

You'll also need to start working on some of the mechanics of book production. Get barcodes (ISBNs), set up accounts with the Library of Congress and the U.S. Copyright Office, and with a printer. You'll also need a system for making sales (yeah!), getting that money in your bank account (yeah, yeah!), and selling your book through various online bookstores.

As if that weren't enough, you'll need to start marketing your book. Even before it exists, you'll need to start building a mailing list. A physical mailing list (mailing addresses) and an electronic list (email list) are both useful.

To do that, you'll need a web page or blog. Depending on your blogging software, your web page might *be* your blog. If you choose to use social media to promote your expertise and your book (highly recommended), then you'll need accounts on Facebook, Twitter, LinkedIn, and other sites relevant to your profession.

If you haven't already done so, you should start speaking to groups about your topic. Once you're published, you'll be able to claim the title "published author." But in the meantime, you're the author of the upcoming book . . ..

Use your speaking opportunities to build your mailing list, get people connected to your blog, etc. All of this builds a following of potential book buyers for the lucky day your books arrive.

At some point, the book comes together and you have two big pieces: the *inside* and the *outside*. The combination of inside and outside is your book. You will upload these to your printer and order proof copies. Proof copies can go to anyone who you think might give you a juicy quote or help promote the book. You should also read through your entire proof copy very carefully before you push the button to approve it.

Before you push the big button, you'll need to finish all those mechanical and sales-related details we discussed. I know it's hard to wait. Use that nervous energy to plan your Launch Party event.

Finally, you decide that you're really, really done with the book. You've got it all set to go. All you have to do is decide how many books to order, based on your budget and expectations. Remember: This is the age of digital printing. You can always order more.

Congratulations: It's a Book! I've never known any author who wasn't excited about the arrival of a new book. Even after a dozen books, I'm still excited when a new book shows up. It's a lot like a baby. And it might have taken longer than nine months to be born!

After the book arrives, just like a baby, you enter a new world. All of your preparation has focused around the birth. Now that it's alive in the world, you need to figure out how to take the next steps to make that book successful.

Some Terminology to Know

As with any other business, publishing has its own language. These words might be familiar to you. Here's what they mean in the book world:

- **Copy Editing** – Many people who are not in the book publishing business confuse copy editing with someone who creates the content of the book (writes the book). "Copy" refers to the words inside the book. A copy editor has the job of making sure all those words are used to have maximum impact. A copy editor will help you to maximize the effectiveness of your writing by making sure that all the "little details" are correct and do not detract from your message.

- **Design** – Design refers to the artistic look and feel of your book. Which fonts will you use? What kinds of drawings or illustrations will you use? How will chapters look? When you have "callouts," what will they look like? How do all of these elements advance the goals of the book?

- **Layout** – As a noun, the layout of a book refers to how it is organized and presented. This includes design features such as illustrations. But primarily, layout refers to the technical side of how the contents of the book are laid out: The placement of margins, page size, headers, footers, fonts/typefaces, and so forth.

- **Layout** – As a verb, to lay out the book is to create a template that integrates all of the design decisions and mechanics. Once completed, the template will allow you to place contents into the book so it will have the look and feel you are seeking.

One final note: Go look at all the books on your shelves. Look at the spines. See what stands out. Where would you put your book? What's to the left and the right of it? What do these kind books look like? What do they *feel* like? What size are they?

Open your books. Look at the title pages. What's there? Now the margins. Get a ruler and measure the margins.

How big are the fonts? Which ones do you like?

How are the books laid out? What do you find most appealing and easy to read? What kind of chapter/section organization do you like?

Are chapter titles informative? Questions? Humorous? Inviting?

What's in the "front matter?" That's the introduction, dedication, foreword, and so forth.

Here's what is really cool about being a book publisher: You get to create whatever book you want. The feel. The texture. The size, the shape. The fonts, the colors, the margins. Everything.

Go consume your books in a whole new way. Lay them out in front of you on the floor and sit with them. They have been your friends and now they get to educate you at a whole new level. Analyze them for the look and the feel and the texture.

. . .

Then begin to building in your mind the perfect, ideal book. Your book. Let's make that happen!

Chapter 5 – Begin with the End In Mind

Earlier I mentioned a bit about expectations. There's a kind of mystery around writing and publishing. We automatically give credibility to someone who has published a book. We somehow see them as successful and smart. They disproportionately represent the people in the front of the room at conferences.

So, with that bias built in, it is very natural that people would believe that they would be successful if they can just publish a book. And while I'm a big believer in leveraging your book so you can move on to bigger things, you need to know that there is no magic in being a published author. Zero. Nada. Zilch.

Sorry.

And let me give you another (unwelcome) dose of reality: Unless you work your butt off, you won't sell many books. Every once in a while I stumble on someone who wrote a book that has become a standard in the industry or required by a government agency. But everyone else has to work for every sale.

Pay attention to the next time a former president writes a book and hits the speaking trail. As long as he's running around from city to city making speeches, the book sells well. As soon as the speaking tour is over, those books are marked down and moved to the closeout table.

Now consider yourself. If the (ex) President of the United States can't sell books without running all over the place speaking to groups, how can you expect to fare any better? Answer: You Can't.

When I talk to authors about selling their books on my technology storefront web site, I ask them what they expect. I tell them to *expect nothing* and be very grateful if they sell something.

If you've done the hard work of building a following, and a mailing list, and a blog, then you have the right to go make speeches and hope that someone recommends your book.

But you probably won't sell thousands, and maybe not hundreds. I know authors who are very proud to have sold 100 copies in a year.

Furthermore, *I* (or Amazon or any online store) can't sell your book if you're not running around creating publicity. When you put yourself out there, speak at industry conferences, blog, Twitter, Facebook, and shout to the world, "Hey! Look at me," then someone will go looking for your book.

If you think that you can put a book up for sale and wait for someone to find it, then you need to know that they never will. No one will ever find your book except by accident.

And they won't buy it unless someone tells them to or it solves their problem immediately. And even then they'll need some poking and prodding.

I don't mean to sound too negative here, but I want to make sure you have realistic expectations. Your book can make you rich. But it will make you rich the same way anything else can make you rich: You have to work really, really hard at it!

My first book sold about 1,000 copies the first year at a profit to me of roughly $65 each. That's $65,000. Not bad. Nothing to sneeze at. Happy to have the money. But that's one year's salary. I don't get to retire because I had one good year in the book business.

And it took me thousands of dollars, a lot of promotion money, and an unbelievable four-country speaking tour to make that happen. Do the math. $90 x 1,000 is $90,000. So I paid out twenty-five thousand dollars to sell those 1,000 books. I had an overhead of $25 per book!

Whether you spend the money on sales commissions, web development, travel expenses, production costs, or Google advertising, you're going to have to shell out something . . . significant . . . in order to make significant book sales.

Now for the good news.

I have written one book as a "work for hire." I got paid a flat fee and then I was done. Let's set that aside. I have also written seven books that I have published myself.

My most successful book has grossed about $400,000 in sales over five years. Every other book has grossed at least $50,000 within the first three years of publication. Most of them have been over the $100,000 mark. That's gross, not profit.

So it can be done. You can make a living at this.

I make a living by writing a minimum of one book per year. And I work my tail off writing, blogging, speaking, training, doing webinars, promoting podcasts, mailing out post cards, begging, pleading, and selling from the front of the room.

My goal is to spend ten years writing one book a year and making an average of $100,000 gross sales per book. At that point I'll see how much "residual" income I can make from those old books. I'm ahead of the goal so far. We'll see how the world turns.

But I have also taken a *huge* percentage of that money and pumped it into a book publishing business. I want to do this for a living.

If you want to sell one book and just sell the heck out of it, you can do that too. There are plenty of people who have built careers around the one book they wrote (or the one book they wrote that anyone cares about).

This chapter is entitled "Begin With the End In Mind." You need to know where you're going before you can get there. You need to have realistic expectations.

Will you sell a million copies? Probably not.

Do you need to sell a million copies? Definitely not.

Play with the math. How much will your book sell for? How can you sell it? Who will you sell it to? How much can you *realistically* make?

In the next two chapters we'll talk about a marketing plan and a business plan. If you are writing and selling your book as a business venture in order to make money, you really need to go through this process. You don't have to do it my way, but you need to do something.

Chapter 6 – Your Marketing Plan

First off, what is a marketing plan? Quite simply, it's the most important tool for determining whether you'll really be able to sell your book. If you write a book proposal for a major publishing house, they're going to want you to answer some very basic questions:

- Who is the audience? Really, honestly, and precisely, who will buy this book?

- How large is this audience? How do you know that?

- How will this audience find out about your book?

- Which other books exist on this topic (or a very similar topic)? Basically, who is the competition?

- How well do competing books sell? How are they sold? How are they priced?

- Given the nature of this audience, the competitive environment, and the pricing of competitive books, how do you think this book should be priced?

You get the picture. It's reality time.

I do some consulting in the areas of marketing and promotion. The most common mistake I see people make is to define their potential audience as *everyone*.

"Everyone needs my book on relationships because everyone *has* relationships." No. It doesn't work like that.

There are plenty of books for whom "everyone" could be the audience. But there is no book – including the Bible, the most widely published book of all time – that has been purchased by everyone.

As strange as it sounds, you will be more successful selling to a smaller audience than to a larger audience. With a smaller audience, you become the expert more easily. Smaller audiences have more communications among themselves. So you can get introduced around more easily. You can become the big fish in a little pond.

Elsewhere (www.promotionmonkey.com) I have spelled out a strategy for creating an audience for yourself among online communities so that you can promote your products. This involves news groups, forums, blogging, web site, social media, email newsletters, and more.

Your marketing plan should lay out what you intend to do in all these areas. It's okay to leave them blank or choose to do nothing in some areas. But where you choose to be active, you need to have a plan. And if it costs money, you need to guess how much it will cost.

One of the big dividing lines in your marketing plan is the book launch. Events and activities are nicely placed before and after the book launch. You don't have to have a specific calendar, but that's not a bad idea.

What will you do leading up to the book launch? Once the book exists and you can start collecting money, what will you do to promote it?

All marketing efforts should be planned and not just haphazard. They should have a known timeframe and a known budget. You should also have some expectation of results. How will you measure those results?

Here's a starter list of items you might use in your marketing:

Marketing Actions

- ✓ Newsletter (email) — Mailed Weekly
- ✓ Blogging — Three Times Per Week
- ✓ Radio Interviews — One Per Month
- ✓ Newsgroups/Forums — Participate 1 Hour Per Week
- ✓ Facebook — 15 mins Per Day
- ✓ Twitter — 15 mins Per Week
- ✓ LinkedIn — 15 mins Per Week
- ✓ Speaking Locally — Once Per Month
- ✓ Speaking Nationally — Once Per Quarter
- ✓ Postcard Campaign — Once at Launch
- ✓ Google Advertising — $5 Per Day
- ✓ Co-Promotion — One Campaign Per Quarter

✓	Ebay Auctions	Five Books at All Times
✓	Give-Aways	One per Amazon Review
✓	Conference Sales	Big Conference One Per Year
✓	Podcast	Once Per Month
✓	Appear on Podcast	Once Per Month
✓	My Webinar	Once per Month
✓	_____	_____
✓	_____	_____
✓	_____	_____

You get the idea. You can also try all kinds of other things. Create postcard advertisements, buy ads on specific web sites, get companies to buy your book and give away, etc.

Remember, for each of these you'll need a budget of some kind (even if it's free) and a way to measure your results. If you blast everything with the only email address or web site you have, how will you know why someone bought or how they heard about you?

Once we get to the discussion of your mailing list software and online store you'll see how you can create custom codes and landing pages. If you give out unique codes for each marketing campaign, you'll be able to measure response rates and return on investment very easily.

I hope you see why the previous chapter was necessary: You need to know that none of this is easy. But it can all be done very systematically and profitably!

The great advantage of measuring what works is that you can repeat what works best and tweak the stuff that didn't work so well.

The beauty of a marketing plan is that you can look at a higher level and see all the activity for a given month, then compare that to the sales for the month.

None of your decisions are etched in stone, so you can fine-tune as you go along. One of the jokes in my office is that my assistant sometimes tells me that I need to go travel more or write another blog post so we can make the rent. She knows that the more I'm out pushing books, the more we sell. When I stop traveling, book sales slow.

If you do decide to take your book to a publisher, having this kind of market analysis and marketing plan will really impress them. Most authors focus on writing and have no idea that they need to be involved in marketing.

Interview: George Sierchio, *B.Y.O.B- Build Your Own Business, Don't Be Your Own Boss*

Q: How have you been able to use your book as a "calling card" for acquiring new business?

A: In my opinion, self-publishing a non-fiction book is the quickest and the most cost effective way to position you and your business as an expert. Since the real point of writing the book is for positioning and marketing, there is no need to take the long, and sometimes non-existent, route of traditional publishing. Making money on the book, in my opinion, is completely secondary since your book is really a big business card.

I think of the costs of a self-published book as part of my marketing budget and use it as a marketing/positioning tool. At speaking engagements or other events, I like to give books away to those that show interest in my company and the knowledge we have. Other times I sell it at a discount as part of another marketing campaign. For some books that are completely digital, I will give them away on my website or as part of a joint venture marketing deal in return for follow up information.

Although it's nice to sell books through a distributor or retail organization, the real use of a book as a marketing tool is to distribute it on your own for free or paid and follow up on your readers. That's how a relationship gets established and enters the reader into your marketing funnel. Distribution avenues will make you a few dollars over the cost of each book, but they don't allow you to capture the name and details of the interested party. When you have a mechanism to capture information, it turns the book from being a PR item into a traceable marketing item to use inside of a true marketing campaign.

George Sierchio, also known as The Consultant's Coach, is an electrical engineer by formal education and a serial entrepreneur by nature.

His coaching and advice revolves around the 4 P's of a successful business (Positioning, Processes, Pricing, Profits) that maximizes money earned and value generated to the business owner. Besides his coaching/advisory work to technology business owners, George is an accomplished speaker, guest university lecturer, frequently contributes to a variety of publications, and has written a number of business related books including *B.Y.O.B- Build Your Own Business, Don't Be Your Own Boss*. His web site is www.actionbusinesspartners.com.

Chapter 7 – Budget and Cash Flow Projection

I almost gave this chapter the title "Realistic Budget and Cash Flow Projection." It's one thing to create a budget. It's another to create a *realistic* budget that will work for your book project.

Most of the un-realism in budgets comes from optimism. Authors assume they'll sell 500 copies the first week, or that every sample copy will result in ten immediate sales. Or they assume that they will always order books in large enough quantities to get great pricing.

In case you haven't put together a budget for a business project before, there's a sample of the format you'll use on the next page.

If you put this into a nice Excel spreadsheet, you can have a column for each month (January, February, March, etc.). That way you can see how projected sales and other income compares to expenses.

To be effective, you need to be really honest with yourself. Sales numbers come from sales reports. All the expenses related to this little business need to be allocated to this project. If you drove two hours to make a speech, you need to track that mileage.

Proposed Budget

Income (January)

	Online Book Sales	$1,000
	On Site Book Sales	$ 500
	Consulting	$ 240
	Speaking	$ 60
Total Income		$ 1,800

Expenses

	Web Site	$ 20
	Store Fees	$ 20
	Travel	$ 320
	Printing	$ 600
	Meals	$ 50
	Advertising	$ 150
	Postage	$ 75
Total Expenses		$ 1,235

Profit (income – expenses) $ 565

Of course, once you religiously track income and outgo from this business, Uncle Sam will view it as a business. So you may be able to take some nice tax deductions for it. Ask your tax pro.

You might also put headers above each month that say "Projected." Then, when you are done settling accounts for the month, you can change that to "Historic." That will give you a realistic comparison between what you think will happen and reality.

As a business consultant, I don't encourage you to revise your projected sales and expenses too often. After all, if you change your projections every time you make a sale, it's really not much of a projection at all.

But every quarter (January, April, July, and October) you can adjust your projections. You need expenses to be very realistic. For example, when you start out you won't have any real idea about the cost of shipping. That will become clearer over time.

After a few months you'll have a sense of whether you're making money – and how much.

This information is great for the spouse who is hoping the investment will pay off, or the relative who loaned you the money to kick off the project in the first place.

In general, if you're going to be in the book business, you need to take care of the *business* piece of the business. A budget with cash flow projection goes a long way in this regard.

Section II: Resources

Chapter 8 – Interns and Other "Staff"

I don't know how big your business is, how many employees you have, or how any of this fits with your standard operating procedures. But if you are an author who has not been running a publishing business, I'm going to assume you're a sole proprietor with no employees. So let me tell you about one of the greatest sources of talent available to you in the creative world: Interns.

Almost all colleges have some kind of internship program. Many high schools as well. Basically, students sign up for an internship "class" and work in your office to earn their school credit. There are some minor forms that have to be signed, stating that the student did the work.

Some internships are unpaid. I prefer to pay because I remember being a student – and because I want these folks to feel like they're part of the team. I start interns at ten dollars per hour. Sometimes I keep them on after the semester is over. From time to time they get a pay increase like everybody else.

I have had great luck with interns from the local design collect and the local community colleges. One intern has become my principle web developer and database administrator.

You can hire interns to design book covers, create internal graphics, create advertising, do the text layout, etc. All the skills you need for the mechanics of creating a book are being taught in college today!

Grow Slow

Let me be very clear on staff: I've got a lot of books out. I have a following in my industry. I have lots of web sites and online stores. In other words, I have the **sales** to support having employees.

When you start out, no matter how successful your book is, you won't be able to hire an office manager, a shipping clerk, two web designers, and an assistant. Someday maybe. But not on day one.

In any business, you'll want to take care of all these chores yourself if you can. But don't be cheap, especially on things like the web site development. Get a great looking, professional online appearance. It will make a lot of difference.

You need help in the production phase of your book. But most of the help you need can be outsourced (see Chapter Ten). So you don't need to hire people for copy editing, layout, etc. Either farm it to an intern or pay someone to do the one job.

After your book is out, you have just a few functions that need attention:

- Marketing / Promotion
- Sales (Online and On Site)
- Shipping
- Keeping Track of Money (Bookkeeping)

Until the profit from your sales is high enough to pay someone to handle one or more of these chores, you'll be doing them yourself.

If you ever get to the point where you hire someone, it will probably be an all-purpose assistant who can manage the books and shipping, and who is sharp enough to help with marketing, promotion, and sales.

Most authors used to be just authors. Now they're authors and publishers. You actually can make more money publishing your own books. But don't spend all your money on staff or you won't have leftovers for yourself!

Even in my business, I could get by with fewer staff. I just happen to run the publishing business as a place to coordinate online stores, speaking engagements, and event management.

It all focuses around selling books. But I make more money from selling advertisements than I make from books. I make more money speaking than I make from books.

But I wouldn't make any of that if I didn't have books.

So the bottom line is to hire staff when you really need them. Put this off as long as possible. Outsource as much as possible. And enjoy being a sole proprietor. That will allow you to focus on being an author instead of an employer!

Chapter 9 – Local Writers / Publishers / Editors

No matter where you live, there are three kinds of groups you should look for: writers, publishers, and speakers. A great place to start looking is meetup.com. That's a web site for people with common interests to organize live in-person meetings.

You'll also find listings in the local paper, on craigslist.org, and through a Google.com search. Local libraries often host these meetings, so you might inquire there as well.

When I first started trying to connect with other authors, I searched for "writers conference" and found both the California Writers Club (see http://calwriters.org/) and the excellent "East of Eden" writers conference, run by one of their branches (see www.southbaywriters.com).

Those links led me to the local chapter of the California Writers Club. From there I met people who were part of the Northern California Publishers and Authors (see www.Norcalpa.org). That group in turn led me to the Independent Book Publishers Association (IBPA – see www.pma-online.org) and The Small Publishers Association of North America (SPAN – see www.spannet.org).

As I met more writers and publishers I found out about a wide variety of local groups. I think you could attend fifteen meetings a month in Sacramento if you wanted to!

Let me point out that most of these are not the kind of clubs where people sit down and critique each other's' writing. There are plenty of those as well, but I'm more interested in the groups that focus on the business side of book publishing. The groups I enjoy the most focus on marketing and the practical side of printing and distribution.

Speakers are a slightly different group. But, as you'll discover, the overlap between authors and speakers is impressive. Over time, many authors find that speaking is a key piece of their marketing strategy. At the same time, professional speakers and trainers have long known that "back of the room sales" can significantly improve your income!

As a general rule, groups for writers and publishers are far more numerous than groups for speakers. In the last five years or so, all of these groups have become more "professional" than they used to be. The explosion of publish-on-demand (POD) and digital printing has made it possible for anyone to be a published author.

Ironically, this trend has made it possible for a lot of *horrible* authors to publish their stuff and for a large number of very good authors to put their work out in the world as never before.

In the "old days" of six or seven years ago, there was a stigma against people who were self-published. The mindset was that your work wasn't good enough to be published by a professional publisher – so it must not be very good. In reality, it just meant that you didn't fit into their business model or promise sales in the range of ten to twenty thousand books.

Now we can see thousands of authors that produce top-quality works that don't fit the old publishing model. Some, like mine, are very "niche-oriented" and expensive. Others are top quality but much short than the publishing houses are willing to promote. It seems that many people have a very good pamphlet in them even if they don't have a full-blown book in them.

Anyway, getting connected to these authors, publishers, and speakers has many benefits. In addition to meeting some very cool people, you will find some great marketing and business connections.

But wait! It gets better. This collection of people will be connected to a larger group across the region and across the country. Every place in America is the home to *someone* who is well known. As you expand your network of "author" connections, you will find people connected to some pretty famous authors.

You'll be amazed at how open these people are to communication – especially if you are respectful and don't abuse their generosity with time. One of the key benefits of this is good old back-of-the-book quote or endorsement.

If you are an expert in your field, then quotes from people known in your field go a long quote. But quotes from famous people never hurt! And if you're not yet established, quotes from famous people can help a lot.

The bottom line: Find groups of people to connect with in your area. It can really boost your business. And there's one more benefit as well: It can be very uplifting and inspiring to meet with people who are eager to share their knowledge. Sometimes being an author is a lonely business – but it doesn't have to be.

Chapter 10 – Outsourcing on the Internet

As you'll see in Section IV, there are a handful of core functions involved in the technical side of producing a book. These include editing, layout, graphics, and creation of the PDF production files. In addition, you might want to format your book for production as an electronic book.

Earlier I mentioned hiring interns or others to help with these functions. Another great alternative is to find these resources on the Internet. After all, the digital age makes practical self-publishing possible. This same digital age connects you with a vast array of talent all over the world.

There are basically three ways to "outsource" using the internet. First, you can find **companies** that do what you need. These might be local, regional, national, or international. They hire lots of people, but you probably only deal with one or two individuals, such as a sales rep and a technician.

Second, you can find **individuals** who are out promoting their services. These folks have web sites, blogs, and mailing lists. They are often connected on social media (Twitter, Facebook, LinkedIn, etc.). You find them by searching for specific keywords or by clicking from blog to blog, web site to web site.

Third, you can use services that **broker** connections between people buying services and people selling services. For example, I have used the site 99Designs.com to have graphics work done. Here's how these "contest" type sites work:

As the "buyer," you start a contest and set the guidelines of what you're looking for. You offer a financial prize. "Sellers" post up their graphics. You give feedback to each entry and the competitors as a group. At the end of the contest, you award the money to someone and they give you all the source files for the artwork.

In all of these options you can find people to:

- Proofread and "copy edit" manuscripts
- Design the book's look and feel
- Design custom graphics, tables, illustrations, etc.
- Create the book cover
- Layout the inside of the book
- Develop marketing plans
- Build web site(s), blog(s), etc.
- Manage your social media presence
- Set up your online store

The biggest challenge to working with people over the Internet is getting used to a non-interactive work environment. You might have occasional phone calls but, most of the time, you'll communicate by email.

I don't recommend sending large or important files by email, although some of that is fine. A much better alternative is a file sharing site that allows you to upload and download files, and to share these with others by sending web links via email.

There are many file sharing services. I use the paid version of Sharefile.com because it allows me to have multiple logons, create folders for different projects, and maintain large libraries of documents "in the cloud."

Anyway, your communication with your virtual helpers will be more *linear* than you are probably used to. But if they are experienced, then they will be able to help you along with the communication.

When you're looking for assistance over the Internet, be sure to ask for references, look at work they've done, and rely on positive referrals if you can. We employers are often tempted to skip these steps in our regular hiring, even though we know we shouldn't. It's even more important that you don't skip these steps when hiring someone over the Internet.

As for taxes, you'll need to work with your accountant. I can give you a few hints, but I'm not an accountant by any stretch of the imagination. I know you need to report payments over $600 per year to the IRS. And when you do that you need to send the person a form 1099. Don't worry, none of that is difficult.

More importantly, these folks are *not* your employees. They are contractors. The federal government has some guidelines about what constitutes an employee vs. a contractor. See www.IRS.gov and search for "Independent Contractor or Employee?"

Basically, if you don't tell the worker how to do their job, when to do it, where to do it, which tools to use, and you don't promise them ongoing work, then you're in good shape. It helps a LOT if you have a written contract. So whether you write it or they write it, a contract that spells out the relationship is normally enough to keep Uncle Sam off your back.

No matter who you use – a company, an individual, or a labor brokering site – you'll want some kind of contract or agreement that spells out a few very important items.

First, you need to make sure it includes a Non-Disclosure Agreement or NDA. An NDA means that they cannot tell anyone about the project or reveal anything they see or read regarding this project. Whenever you delve into the world of intellectual property, you need an NDA.

Second, you need to make sure that any products or services created by the other party become *your property*. Some sites, such as 99designs.com, actually hold your payment in escrow until you verify that the artist has transmitted all the artwork and related files to you, and released the copyright to you.

Third, as with any other work for hire, you need to spell out as specifically as you can what you expect to see as a final product or service, and what you intend to pay for the product or service.

Generally speaking, I have found it extremely easy to work with people who offer their services over the Internet. They have a standard routine. They know they need to communicate a certain way to be successful, and they know that referrals will make or break their business.

The woman who did the layout work on my first three books lives in Seattle, WA. I have never met her. My favorite copy editor lives in my hometown of Sacramento, CA. I've only met her once face to face, and that was after she's finished the first major project for me.

Working with Internet-based businesses is easy and can give you access to some excellent talent you might not run into on the local job scene.

For more information on hiring a "Virtual Assistant" (individual or company), see the interview with Sharon Broughton at the end of this chapter.

Crowdsourcing On The Internet

Crowdsourcing means asking the people you're connected to on the Internet to contribute to your work. The most effective way for you to use this is to get feedback.

On Yahoo Groups, Google Groups, Facebook, Twitter, and wherever you hang out, there are people who can give you feedback. The great thing about these "communities" is that they will fulfill simple requests very quickly.

For example, when I was getting ready to publish my first book, I created a Yahoo Group that was private and just for that group. I posted up possible titles and subtitles, cover designs, and so forth. Today I would do all of that on Facebook.

In addition to getting good feedback very quickly, you can use this kind of crowdsourcing to start to build some buzz about your book. For my Yahoo Group, I rewarded my small band of helpers with a free copy of the final product.

Interview: Sharon Broughton, The Techie VA

Q: How can a Virtual Assistant make life easier for a new book publisher?

A: They can help you with research, layout, minor editing and proofreading, online marketing, social marketing, setting up your shopping cart, designing an email newsletter, building a website and keeping the marketing ball rolling.

Some virtual assistants are super techie and can set up your shopping cart, design your website, set up your social networking profiles and develop a launch plan for you and then implement it. Other virtual assistants are generalists and can help you set up book signings, send out press releases, distribute articles, and update your blog posts.

Q: What is the cost for a VA?

A: *Prices for virtual assistants range from $6 to $100 per hour. Be sure to pick the right virtual assistant for the job.*

Q: Any tips on how to manage a team, including any virtual professionals you hire?

A: *My favorite tip for authors is to make sure that there are clear expectations and deadlines with everyone on your team. I highly recommend using an online project management tool. Some of my favorites are Central Desktop (www.centraldesktop.com), Basecamp (www.basecamphq.com) and TeamworkPM (www.teamworkpm.net). Most of these services have free options so you can try them out before buying. They all let you set up milestones and task lists (one for marketing, one for writing the book, etc.). You can invite all the team members to the tool and assign tasks and deadlines. It really helps keep everyone on task.*

For specific links to Virtual Assistants, see the Resources section.

Sharon Broughton is the owner of The Techie VA (www.thetechieva.com), an online training company that teaches virtual assistants the technical aspects of being a VA. Sharon also has her own virtual assistant business, Sharon Broughton Team (www.sharonbroughtonteam.com), that specializes in online marketing plans and implementation, shopping cart setup and maintenance, product, book and event launches, web and ezine design and more.

Section III: Some Mechanics and Technical Stuff

Chapter 11 – Legal and Tax Issues

There are only a few points to cover here, but they're worth a bit of time. I have a separate chapter on copyrights. That's the most important legal aspect of publishing!

If you are just "you," then publishing is a little easier. But if you have other businesses, or your business life is complicated in any way, then you might consider creating a legal entity to publish your book. This might be an S-Corp, LLC, or some other option.

There are two reasons to spend a little time on this. First, if you personally have an estate of any kind that needs to be protected, then an S-Corp or some other entity can isolate you and your personal belongings from your business venture into the world of book publishing.

Second, if your publishing activities turn into a nice, big, profitable business, then you'll want to have a legal, taxable entity that can help you write off some of your expenses so that they are not taxable. As a general rule, S-Corps have evolved to be the vehicle of choice for this sort of thing.

You might not want to create a separate legal entity right away. Talk to your tax professional (Enrolled Agent or CPA) about whether, and when, you might want to incorporate. As the owner of more than one S-Corp, I draw the line in the range of $50,000 to $60,000 in *profit* (not income).

If that seems like a lot of money, it's because it is!

Most books will never have that kind of profit. But I'm hope that yours will . . . with the help of this book. <wink> I know that I expect that kind of profit every year, and I work hard to make it happen.

Warnings and Notices

First off: Fair Warning. I'm not a lawyer. I'm not a tax professional, so take all my advice with a grain of salt and consult a professional. Having said that . . .

Luckily, there aren't many legal matters to worry about with non-fiction. And pretty much all of them can be taken care of with a paragraph like the one above. Depending on the kind of information you are doling out, you may need to be more specific about your warning.

For example, I have a book on Service Agreements (contracts) for technical consultants. It discusses service agreements/contracts, and even has sample contracts. But, as I said, I'm not a lawyer. So I make it very clear that the reader should not just take my template and shove it in front of a client.

In fact, I go well beyond that. I have a footer on every page of the template that says "You should have a lawyer review every agreement or contract you sign." Even if you *were* an attorney and you wrote a book like this, you'd want to put that warning in there. Laws are different in every state, and they change constantly.

Depending on the advice you give in your book, you might want to craft some kind of notice to put in the "front matter" of your book. That means in the introduction, the foreword, or some other place at the beginning.

For the most part, most people have common sense. And, interestingly enough, other people will be inspired by your book but take actions that you would never dream of. So the only people who are really a potential problem is the very tiny group that takes your advice verbatim, has no common sense, implements it, somehow manages to mess up their business, AND gets an attorney to agree to blame it on you.

I have never actually heard of this happening, but we live in a litigious society. So, depending on what kind of advice you give, you might find a warning useful. In my recent *Network Migration Workbook*, I conclude the Legal Warning by simply stating, "And finally: You're responsible for what you do."

If you believe you should have some sort of warning, begin by looking at other books in your field to see the kinds of legal statements and liability warnings they include. To be honest, most don't include anything, even if they're giving information that could be very damaging if used incorrectly.

So, take this stuff seriously. But don't lose sleep over it. Put together a good paragraph, have it reviewed by an attorney, and move on.

Sales Tax

Finally, you may have to deal with Sales Tax. Every state is different. For states without sales tax, there may be another permit required to sell products. Go figure it out.

If your state does have sales tax, you are probably in for a surprise with regard to how complicated the government can make things. In most states with a sales tax there are multiple layers of tax. There's a state component and a county component. In some areas there's a school district component, a city component, and then special districts. There are special districts for roads, mass transit, libraries, water districts, and pretty much anything you can think of.

So, for example, in California, there are over 100 different unique combinations of sales taxes. It all adds up to somewhere between 7% and 9% of most people. But as a reseller, I need to keep track of sales in every single district.

Note: None of this is advice of any kind . . . except my advice to contact your accountant to make sure your financial butt is covered.

When I make sales over the Internet inside California, I need to collect sales tax. But if I make sales to other states, I don't collect it.

When I travel to other states I am supposed to collect the sales tax and pay it to that state. But the dollars involved in such transactions are really pennies. So, to be honest, I don't make an attempt to deal with this unless the sales are huge. I don't want to waste $300 in labor to pay $5 in taxes.

You have to decide what you want to do on this front. But just educate yourself first. Seller beware.

Chapter 12 – ISBNs

Your book is unique, like a snowflake. But as you'll see in Chapter 15, titles aren't copyrighted. For this and many other reasons, each book must have a unique numeric identifier. We call this an ISBN or International Standard Book Number.

If you want a deep dive on ISBNs, start at http://www.isbn.org. You'll quickly find yourself at https://www.myidentifiers.com, which is the home for "all things ISBN" in the United States.

Each country has a different organization for assigning ISBNs. You must obtain an ISBN for the agency in which your business is located.

ISBNs are assigned to publishers. If you obtain ISBN numbers yourself (which I *highly* recommend), then they will always be associated with your publishing business. If you receive an ISBN that is "resold" to you by another publisher, then your book will be associated with that publisher.

Each book, and each edition, must have a unique identifier. This makes it possible to know exactly which product is being bought, sold, shipped, etc.

Until 2007, ISBNs were 10 digits long. Now they are 13 digits long. The first round of ISBN numbers to be published as 13-digit numbers in the U.S. were those beginning with 978. As of the publication of this book, 978 numbers are still being issued.

In order to maintain compatibility with older systems, there are utilities that convert 978 numbers into "equivalent" 10-digit ISBN codes. You probably don't need to do this or worry about it. For several years now I have produced books that only displayed the newer 13-digit (978) ISBNs.

When the 978 numbers are depleted, then the 979 series will be issued. 979 numbers will not convert to a 10-digit equivalent. Again, I don't have a use for the older numbers now, so I don't foresee this as an issue several years from now.

Bowker is the name of the company that manages the ISBN registration services in the U.S. Once you register your publishing company at https://www.myidentifiers.com, you will be able to purchase ISBNs from that site. As of Summer 2011, the cost is $125 for a single ISBN and $250 for a block of ten. Get the block of ten.

The cost is minimal and you might as well have them. After all, you'll need a different ISBN for every version of the book. That means the ebook version is different from the printed version. The 2nd Edition is a different book from the 1st Edition. And the ebook version for Kindle is different from the ebook version for the Nook reader. So just buy the 10-pack.

At the end of this chapter is a list of things that get (and don't get) ISBNs. Please note:

An ISBN number can never be reused. Period.

Some printers offer to sell you their ISBNs to put on your book. Unless you have a very good reason to do this, *don't do this*! First, it is a sign to everyone in the supply chain that you are an amateur and a self-published author. If you only intend to sell from the web site at that printing house, fine. But if you intend to distribute more widely, you'll need your own ISBN.

As you see in Chapter 22, the largest book distributor in the world is Ingram Books. If you print your own books (have them printed), you can sell them through many channels. But you *can't* sell them through Ingram Books unless you have at least ten book titles in your catalog. So, one strategy is to figure out how you can get ten titles. If nothing else, you'll need a block of ten ISBNs to assign to books for this undertaking.

But even if you have your book printed by Lightning Source (the print-on-demand arm of Ingram Books that gets you in their catalog with only one title), you'll still need your own ISBN to assign to the book.

Bottom line: Buy a block of ten.

ISBN Graphics

You've seen the barcode on the back of just about every book you've ever purchased. It's the set of long black and while lines that looks something like this:

ISBN 978-0-9763760-0-2

In addition to the 13-digit ISBN number, you can encode the suggested retail price of the product. That little bit appears to the right of the ISBN itself as a smaller numeric barcode.

There are lots of programs for generating these codes as graphics files. If you use one that you found out on the Internet, make sure that it produces a high resolution graphic. A TIFF format is best.

Basically, you want to avoid something in a 300 dpi (dots per inch), low-resolution format. It will look bad, scan poorly, and may cause you problems with your printer.

As a rule, you can just get the graphic when you buy your ISBNs and keep track of them. The ISBN above is in a file called

Relax Focus Succeed book_978-0-9763760-0-2__001.tif

I could have just called it "978-0-9763760-0-2__001.tif" but I like the human-readable component. It keeps me from making stupid mistakes.

Note: Some printers, including Lightning Source, give you the option to include the ISBN graphic in the template they generate for you when you use their (free) book cover template generator. Because it's already embedded in the template they send you, you know it will look great on the book.

If for whatever reason you had your books printed without an ISBN, you can use the graphic to have nice labels made. With luck, you at least left a nice place on the back of the book to put your ISBN. If you go this route, have the ISBN code printed on coated, glossy labels that won't get scuffed in shipping.

What ISBNs are *Not*

Please note that an ISBN is not a "barcode" as we normally use that term. Strictly speaking, an ISBN is a number. It's the number that represents your book as it winds its way through ordering, shipping, warehousing, and delivery. The graphic we're familiar with is just a barcode that reflects the numeric information.

ISBNs are not the same as UPCs (Uniform Product Codes), EANs (European Article Numbers), or any other "barcode" graphics that exist in the world of retail. Many industries have their own number systems for tracking items. ISBNs are simply the codes used with books.

What Gets an ISBN?

Many items can use an ISBN if you intend to sell them beyond your own web site. The list of what gets an ISBN changes slowly, but it does change over time. To the best of my knowledge this is accurate information. For the latest information, see http://www.isbn.org.

These items need an ISBN:

- Audiobooks
- Brochures and pamphlets
- Cell phone novels
- Coloring books
- Graphic novels
  (Note: comic books do not get an ISBN because they are serials)
- Historical documents
- Loose-leaf volumes
- Maps
- Podiobooks
- Puzzle books

These items are not assigned an ISBN:

- Advertising and promotional materials
- Blogs
- Board games
- Calendars
- Clothing
- Coffee mugs and other utensils
- Comic books
- Compact Discs (CDs and DVDs). Music or performance CDs are not assigned ISBNs. Meditation CDs that combine music and spoken word are not assigned ISBNs.
- Digital customized publications
- Electronic advertising / promotional materials
- Electronic newsletters / e-zines
- Electronic schedulers
- Electronic/video games
- Food and medicine No
- Greeting cards. Greeting cards are not assigned ISBNs unless required by the retailer. If assigned, they are assigned by price point rather than design. For example, if several different designs are all sold for the same price, only one ISBN is used.
- Magazines No (see Serials)
- Music/performance CDs No (see Compact discs)
- Online databases No, publications subject to frequent update (online databases, blogs, etc.) are not eligible for ISBNs.

- Periodicals
- Personal documents, if digitized
- Pictures and photographs
- Playing cards and tarot cards
- Postcards
- Posters and art prints
- Search engines No
- Serials (magazines, periodicals, etc.)
- Sheet music
- Shirts and other apparel
- Stationery items
- Toys, including stuffed animals
- Web-based games

And of course there are a few things that may get an ISBN under the right circumstances:

- Journals and diaries can be assigned ISBNs when required by retailers
- Chapters, paragraphs, and other small sections of published text may be assigned an ISBNs if they are being sold separately
- Compact Discs (CDs and DVDs) may be assigned ISBNs if they are spoken word or instructional
- Flash cards may be assigned an ISBN if they are instructional in nature. Playing cards and tarot cards are not eligible for ISBNs.

- Software may be assigned an ISBN if it is educational or instructional

Note that these are not complete lists of "yes/no/maybe" regarding ISBNs. If you have something other than a book, please do your research and determine what's appropriate.

Chapter 13 – Some Design Considerations

It doesn't matter how technical you are: You have to know a few things about the mechanics of your book. If you're going to do all the work yourself, this chapter will give you a few things to watch out for. If you're going to hand it off to someone else, then have them read this chapter for you.

As an author, when you create a book, you want to think in terms of words and ideas. But as a publisher you need to begin to think about the practical side of creating something that's pleasant to experience as a reader. At some point your ideas need to be transformed into an attractive, readable experience.

One of the great weaknesses of "modern" technology is that anyone can create a bad book. But with a little attention to detail, you can also create an attractive book that's (literally) easy on the eyes.

The problem – and the promise – come from the fact that we all have computers and it's so easy to create something. But creating *something* isn't good enough. You want to create something that is designed so your technical capabilities are not on parade. In other words, don't get too fancy, and don't be too plain.

Whoever does your layout work should read a book or two on book design. One that I found particularly good for beginners is *Book Design and Production* by Pete Masterson.

Some of the biggest mistakes made by self-publishers have to do with the most visible elements of the book. These include the big three: Fonts, Layout, and Graphics.

Fonts

In the good old days before we all had computers, the art of type-setting was taken very seriously. Now we can select-all and click on a different font. Done. We can make microscopic changes to font size. We can make the font uncomfortably large or small.

You should choose one primary font for your book. It should be very easy to read. This is *not* the time to get fancy or worry about being on the cutting edge. You can add design elements to show how cool you are. The font or typeface for your text should be chosen because it is readable.

For the most part, you will want to choose a font that is either in the family of fonts similar to Times Roman (a serif font) or Arial (a sans-serif font). Some people argue that those two fonts are over-used. That's why I say something like them.

Times Roman is universally considered the most *readable* font. The font I am using for this book is called *Minion Pro*

Medium. It is copyrighted by Adobe and I have purchased a license to use it. As you can see, it is very much in the Times Roman family.

You can buy fonts for your books from many places. They range in price from under $100 to several hundred dollars. I don't recommend a cheap font for your book because you don't know what problems you'll have with the printers. Either use a font that ships with your computer or buy a good one.

You can use different fonts (including super-cool fonts) for headers, footers, chapter titles, section headings, illustrations, and so forth. You can even use serif fonts for these despite the fact that your primary font is sans-serif. The choice of fonts is a design component, so be careful which combinations you come up with.

Do not use more than three different fonts in your book unless you really know what you're doing. It really sucks to have a book come off the press and look like a ransom note!

The biggest mistake I see with digital printing is that people use fonts that are too small. I don't know if they are trying to save space and print fewer pages or what. This can be very bad. My life coach recommended a book to me which I bought. But after working my way through two chapters I told her I just couldn't finish it. The type gave me a headache. When readers are squinting, the font is getting in the way of actually reading the book.

In another instance, a friend of mine published a book with a slightly smaller font. It was still very readable, but he did not adjust the line spacing. The result was that the book looked almost (but not quite) double-spaced. Again, this was very distracting.

Layout

Layout refers to the actual placement of text and other "elements" on the page. It takes into consideration each element, such as headers, paragraphs, illustrations, tables, and so forth.

The biggest problems with layout have to do, again, with making the page readable. As strange as this sounds, margins matter. White space matters. How text moves around graphics matters. Everything matters. In a well laid-out book, you won't notice any of these things because they will all work together for the common good. In an amateur publication, your attention is drawn away from the message and onto the messenger (the layout).

Margins, for example, are not even all around in a book. That would look strange. You need to take into consideration the internal and external spacing. The inside margin has to be large enough to read comfortably when the pages are opened.

Another hidden culprit in bad layout is an old word processor. If you are using a dedicated layout tool such as InDesign or Adobe PageMaker, then you can make all kinds of adjustments to type spacing. If you have a newer version of Microsoft Word (Newer means 2007 or newer), then it does a pretty good job.

But if you have an older version of Word, WordPerfect, or any other "word processor" that was not intended as a layout tool for books, then you will have problems that can't be fixed. Even the things you can adjust, such as kerning (the way horizontal space between letters is managed) are not easily adjusted. It is cheaper to buy the right tool for the job than to spend hours and hours adjusting things and hoping you don't have to repaginate.

For example, when an old version of Word puts spaces between words, it is not very sophisticated. And if you add extra spaces for tabs, or after periods, then you'll see rivers of white running up and down the pages of your book. Just like awkward margins or small fonts, this layout "flaw" draws attention to itself and away from your brilliant ideas.

Justifying the right side of your text makes this worse. Unless you have really good, modern software, and you know how to use it, don't "full justify" your text.

Graphics

The first rule of graphics is that you have to start out with really high resolution. That means you can almost never just grab stuff you happen to have handy and use it. One of the online services I use sets *minimum* sizes for graphics, and their minimums are huge. They're not worried about maximums because they're not worried about file size.

During the process of formatting your files, creating PDFs (see next topic), and printing, you're going to lose a little bit of detail at each stage. So you want to start out with as much detail as possible. If you start out with something low resolution (e.g., 300 DPI), it's going to look like garbage on the printed page. Some printers won't even accept it.

Unless you have a reason to print color graphics on the inside of your book (for example, a coffee table book), you will be using black and white, and gray scale, on the interior. You'll need to work with a graphic artist to either convert your graphics or determine that they look great in gray scale and don't need to be converted.

Graphics are generally good for you book. On many subjects they are necessary. At a minimum, they can be diverting and a nice change of pace. So the message is to use graphics. But again, use them sparingly. Use them to contribute to the overall layout design. And don't let them detract from your message.

PDFs

PDF stands for Portable Document Format, a layout standard originally designed by Adobe Systems. It is now an open standard, meaning that lots of other companies are designing software around this format.

The PDF standard was designed so that you could exchange documents between computers using different hardware, different operating systems, and different software . . . and it would always look the same. Each PDF document contains all the data needed to recreate two dimensional graphics, text, and fonts.

This is such a universally successful file format that virtually any printer you sent your book to will insist on a PDF document. In fact, they'll insist on two PDF documents: One for the outside cover and one for the inside contents.

Along with your PDF document, you'll need to send all the fonts you used and all the hi-res graphics you used.

Important Safety Tip: Store a copy of your fonts and hi-res graphics with your book documents so that you will have them when you need to send them to the printer!

With many printers, you can send a file with the fonts embedded. That means that all the information needed to reconstruct your fonts will be built into the PDF file. This is handy, *but you have to know how to do it.* The process is different in different programs, so you'll have to make sure you (or whoever creates the files) know what you're doing.

Advice

We'll revisit this topic again in the next section. For now, just one final piece of advice: Take advice! Ask other people what they think, and then beat them up so they give you the truth. People are often amazed that someone is actually going through the process of producing a book. As a result, they love it all.

Right now you don't need love. You need to put on your professional armor and forget the fact that you invested 50 hours in a graphic. If everyone you talk to says it looks like garbage, or it look amateurish, then get rid of it.

Remember those local writers I introduced you to in Chapter Nine? Find a bunch of them and take them to lunch. Ask them how it looks. Ask them what they'd do.

You can either choose your ego or professional success. Pick one. If you decide to go with professional success, you'll get rid of, or change, whatever doesn't work. And you'll end up with a *more* professional, *more* successful book.

So seek advice and then take it.

Chapter 14 – Library of Congress

I don't want to get too political here, but if you're looking for a government agency that actually works really hard to serve the people it is chartered to serve, then you're going to love the Library of Congress. When in doubt, go to

http://www.loc.gov/publish/

and you'll be amazed at how thorough the site is. And it's easy to understand as well!

Open up the title page of most books that are professionally published and you'll find something called the Cataloging in Publication Program (CIP) and Catalog Card Number. See http://cip.loc.gov/process.html for more information.

These are things that librarians use to locate specific Library of Congress catalog records in the national databases. They use this information to order catalog cards from the Library of Congress and to order books from commercial suppliers.

Important Safety Tip: The LOC (Library of Congress) assigns a CIP number *before* the book is published. T One of the old beliefs about copyright is his way, the information can be printed on the title page of the book once it is published. The goal here is to make it easier for book dealers and librarians to buy your book.

Basically, the process consists of these steps:

1. You send an application along with an electronic copy of your book to the LOC
2. You are assigned a LOC Control Number (Preassigned Control Number of PCN)
3. The LOC determines the appropriate category, sub-category, Dewey Decimal designation (I'm not kidding here), and LOC catalog number
4. You (the publisher) receive this information so you can print it on the copyright page
5. A machine-readable "official" description of your book is distributed to large libraries, bibliographic utilities, and book vendors around the world
6. You send a copy of your work (book) to the LOC. They verify that all the information is accurate and add some information to the previous electronic record (for example, final page count).
7. LOC updates the book's electronic records with the latest information

Once you create a logon at http://cip.loc.gov/, you'll be able to use that for future books as well.

Your Library of Congress catalog card number should appear on the copyright page of your book. If you can manage to include this catalog number in book reviews, it allows subscribers to the Library of Congress catalog service to order cards by number and eliminate a search fee. If you plan to sell to libraries, you must have an LOC number.

Please note: a Library of Congress registration and LOC catalog number are not required to sell your book. But they open up some pretty big markets, and the process is easy. I recommend that you do this.

Notes On The Process

Once you create a login at LOC.gov, you'll go to http://pcn.loc.gov to actually enter information for you book. The site is *very* old-school. It literally looks like one of the first web sites on the Internet in in 1994 and hasn't been updated since. But it works.

Follow the links to the PCN Application. You'll need to have the following information:

- Title
- Sub-Title
- Edition (if appropriate)
- Publisher
- City / State
- Author name for up to three authors
- Editor name for up to three editors
- Approximate number of pages

- If you plan more than one volume, how many additional volumes do you expect?
- Is this a periodical?
- The ISBN for this title. Use the format 978-0-9819978-4-1 not 9780981997841.
- Qualifier (hardcover, paperback, diskette, answer book, volume 1, etc.)
- If the paper is acid-free, check the "permanent paper" box. If you don't know this, leave it blank.
- Primary language if other than English
- Is the book intended for children or young adults?
- Series title, if appropriate
- Month of Publication
- Email address where the PCN will be sent
- You contact information

Click Submit and wait up to a week (For this book the process took about fifteen minutes). If you have changes to the information you submitted, you need to wait until you have a PCN and then enter a change request.

You will receive an email with your Control Number.

Once you receive a control number, try to use it in you publicity so that interest book sellers can easily order your book.

Interview: William C. Teie, *Firefighter's Handbook on Wildland Firefighting*

Q: What's the most important thing you wish you'd known when you produced your first book?

A: There are three elements of publishing that I wish I had known: (1) That it is the author's responsibility to market his or her book, regardless if you self-publish or have someone else publish the book for you; (2) That there is a big difference between the price a book sells for and the amount that the author or publisher gets to keep. Unless your name is Clancy or King, someone else makes the money; and (3) That if your book isn't priced right, discounts will destroy any potential for profit.

The key is that any new author or potential self-publisher MUST fully understand the process, or they will get some surprises that will ruin their day!

Q: How has the Internet changed your publishing business?

A: First, the Internet is a researcher's best friend; all you have to do is 'Google it!' But, its potential ability to market to the World is scary. Any new self-publisher must spend the time and learn this new model.

Q: How many different printers have you used and what made you settle on your current printer?

I have used several printers over the years, but have found two that I now use exclusively. The one I use locally prints all of the one- or two-color products. I have used them for over 15 years. I trust them and don't even get bids from anyone else. They do quality work, and market prices and stand behind their work. For all of the four-color work I use another printer, based in China. I don't like going off-shore, but to keep the price of the final product competitive, I have to. Again, I use only one printer ... for the same reasons listed above.

Q: What other advice do you have for people who are working to publish their first book?

A: It is the author's responsibility to write a book that someone ELSE wants and is willing to pay for. Study your potential customers and understand what it is that will make their lives easier. Give the potential customer quality and tools toward an end, be that entertainment, education or technology. Do not trust your ability to edit or proofread, you are too close to the information—let a professional do that stuff—and don't shoot the messenger if you don't like what they do. This doesn't mean you don't control them; they are working for you, but listen to what they suggest.

Get a passion for what you want to do, then do it. You can't sell half-done books for very long. Take the time to do it right, for the right reasons, and enjoy. Most of your rewards will come in the form of "psychic income," that can fill your heart and put a smile on your face.

William C. Teie retired from the California Department of Forestry and Fire Protection (CAL FIRE) after a successful 34-year career. He worked up through the ranks from seasonal firefighter to Deputy Director for Fire Protection. In this position, he was responsible for all of the fire protection programs within CAL FIRE.

Chief Teie was very active in the California fire service. He was on the Board of Directors of the California Fire Chiefs Association, and was President in 1986-87. He is also a charter member of the USA branch of the Institute of Fire Engineers.

He is the author and publisher of the *Firefighter's Handbook on Wildland Firefighting, Fire Officer's Handbook on Wildland Firefighting, Leadership for the Wildland Fire Officer, Wildland Firefighting Fundamentals*, the series of *Fire in the West* reports, and has developed several training and operational aids for the firefighter. In 2004, two of his books were published in South Africa; the *Fire Manager's Handbook on Veld and Forest Fires* and the *Veld and Forest Firefighting Fundamentals*.

You can learn more about Bill and his publications at www.deervalleypress.com.

Chapter 15 – Copyrights

I mentioned earlier that most of the "legal" stuff related to books is in the copyright. Well here we are. Luckily, copyrights are a lot easier to understand than most people suspect.

Basically, you own your copyright just by claiming it.

> Copyright © 2011 Karl W. Palachuk

Note: Some book printers and publishers are very picky about the format of that line. The U.S. Copyright Office is a lot more forgiving. Better safe than sorry. Do it however your printer wants it.

One of the old beliefs about copyright is that you have to prove that you wrote something, so you should send a copy to yourself in an envelope so it would come back with a date stamped on it.

These days, with the Internet and computers, you've got date stamps all over the place. Once you publicly display your work, you own the copyrights to it. Period.

But then there's the matter of copyright infringement. You *should* (in my opinion) officially copyright your work in the off chance that someone violates your copyright. If you have to sue someone for damages, life is much easier if you have your copyright registered with the Copyright Office.

First, you can sue for related "damages," but you cannot sue for *copyright infringement* in a U.S. court without copyright registration. Second, if your work is registered before publication, or within five years of publication, the act of copyright registration is accepted by the courts as prima facie evidence that you are the copyright holder.

This means that, if you ever go to court, a judgment in your favor is almost automatic.

If copyright registration is made prior to an infringement of the work, statutory damages and attorney's fees will be available to the copyright owner in court actions. Otherwise, only an award of actual damages and profits is available to the copyright owner.

The copyright office listed at the end of this chapter is a great resource and has a process for electronically registering your copyright.

Five Copy Rights

If you go to sell (or even protect) your copyright, be aware that there are five exclusive rights within the concept of "copyright." They are:

    (1) The right to reproduce (make copies) of the work

(2) The right to license or sell the work to others

(3) The right to create derivative works from the original works (these include second editions, multiple revisions, translations, sound recordings, etc. and could include a new book with a lot of similar material, depending on how much you use of the original work)

(4) The right to publicly display the work

(5) The right to publicly perform the work

The copyright owner is permitted to sell or license all or only a portion of these rights. Any sale or license you grant to another must be carefully defined. If you simply say, "sell or license the copyright," it could be construed that you have given away all of your rights, including your right to create derivative works (or second editions).

If you want to retain the right to create derivative works (second editions and new books using a lot of the original material), you must either (i) carefully craft your sale or license agreement to make it narrow enough to not include these rights, or (ii) reserve these rights to yourself.

Note: Like all legal issues, none of this is important until it's very important!

Luckily, the Copyright Office is within the Library of Congress. See http://www.copyright.gov/.

You may register a copyright while the book is in manuscript form (not printed) or after the book is printed. You simply send in a copy of the book along with a form and a fee.

I recommend that you get your ducks in a row and take care of the copyright process as soon as the book is essentially complete. That way you can put official information on your copyright page with the first printing.

A Few More Notes On Copyright

I'm not sure where else to put this, so here it is for completeness.

1. You cannot copyright a title. So you could write a book called *The Grapes of Wrath*. Now you might not sell six copies, but you can legally give your book that title.

This is important because it means that you need to be aware of your title. I have a business called Relax Focus Succeed®. Notice that registered trademark there? I somehow got a trademark on that title for my business. So I can use it as my title and be very confident that no one will be able to write a similarly-named book.

Be aware that you cannot write a book that infringes on someone else's rights, even if they can't copyright the title. They still have rights they can protect. Don't tempt fate.

That being said, if you come up with a great title that is not a protected business name, but *is* a book title, you can re-use that title. This is primarily a marketing decision you'll have to make.

2. Some written works are in the *Public Domain*, which means that no one can claim right to them because we all own them.

You can reprint works in the public domain. You can't claim them as your own, but you can reprint them and not have to pay the original author or publisher.

For example, I can reprint anything Charles Dickens wrote. If I add something original, like my layout and my introduction, then I can copyright that production of that book. And no one could legally copy my production.

This is why you see whole bookshelves full of store-brand reprints of the classics: It cost essentially nothing to produce them.

Now you might not have a use for reprinting old, no-longer-copyrighted material. But you should know that it exists and is available as a resource if you need it.

I won't go into the details of what is and is not eligible for use in this manner. If you have a use for such material, start by looking at the Library of Congress publications "How to Investigate the Copyright Status of a Work." This is found here: http://www.copyright.gov/circs/circ22.pdf

Here are a few links:

> http://www.copyright.gov/

E-filing of copyrights for e-products:

> http://www.copyright.gov/register/index.html

Regarding the topic of automatic penalties and related protections see

> http://www.copyright.gov/circs/circ1.pdf

Section IV: Editing, Layout, and Production

Chapter 16 – Layout

There are three **monstrous mistakes** made by amateurs and first-time self-publishers. The first of these is the layout. If you don't know what you're doing, and you don't hire someone who knows what they're doing, then you have very little chance of creating a good looking, professional book.

By now you've seen the term "layout" several times in this book, as both a noun and a verb. When it comes to production, layout is really where ideas become reality. This is where the actual book comes into existence.

After you've written a few books you'll feel much more comfortable with the various aspects of layout. For your first book, I highly recommend that you work with someone who's done it before. See Section II on Resources.

Having said that, I also encourage you to be involved in all the decisions about how your book is laid out. Part of this is a design function, and part is a very practical decision making process.

Your book has three major pieces, one much larger than the others. First, you have the "front matter," which includes the title page, copyright page, table of contents, dedication, foreword, "About the Author," preface, and maybe a legal note that you're not responsible for anything you do.

Depending on your style and what seems right, you may not have all of these. As a non-fiction writer, I prefer to use Chapter One as an introduction, so I don't use a preface.

Some of the front matter is very practical. This includes the title page, copyright information page (which includes Library of Congress information, ISBN numbers, etc.), and the table of contents. Most of the rest of the front matter is either self-serving (acknowledgements, dedication) or simply serves to warm up the reader so they get a sense of the project they hold in their hands.

I take my front matter seriously since it's often the most personal part of a non-fiction book. But I also realize that almost no one will ever read it. That's a little sad to think about. But hey, I rarely spend a lot of time on other people's front matter. Reality, baby.

The second major part of your book is the chapters. This is normally the largest part of the book. Once in a while you'll produce something with a huge amount of material as an appendix, but this is uncommon. Your chapters are the biggest, most important part of your book.

Perhaps the most important thing to consider when you lay out your chapters is that you need to **break it up**! That means *please* do something interesting so you don't have 300 pages of text. Here are a few things you can do:

- Add white space at the top of chapters
- Use lists (like this)
- Add tables and illustrations when appropriate
- Write "side bar" articles that highlight a point
- Add quotes at appropriate points
- Insert interviews (as I've done in this book)
- Use different font sizes

The basic idea is that you need to make design decisions that break up the monotony of text, text, never-ending text. You might be the most thrilling author in the world, but in a non-fiction work, it's very important to create a "whole" project that feel accessible to the reader. Hundreds of pages of block text does not accomplish this!

Inside Basics

If you've poured over books in fine detail, then you should have a sense of the look and feel that you want. But you also need to consider the basics of the technical side of book production. For example, notice that professional book have the odd numbered pages on the right side. If you want to look like an amateur, mess this up!

Traditionally, new chapters have started on odd numbered pages simply because they're on the right side. That means you might have an occasional blank page. Don't worry about it. White space is your friend.

You'll also need to decide what to include in the headers and footers of your pages. If you're used to using a word processor (e.g., Microsoft Word), then you're probably familiar with one header and one footer, or maybe a different header/ footer combination on the first page of a document.

In a book you actually have four places to put information: The top left, the top right, the bottom left, and the bottom right. You can put the same information in all headers and footers, but you should decide what you want to do.

Information you should put somewhere in these spaces includes the page number and the book title. You may also choose to put the chapter title or section headings in the headers or footers.

Another option is to put non-traditional information here. I love to put my web site in the footer of most books. This is particularly good if the web site provides additional services or products for the most likely readers. As I mentioned earlier, I have also put legal notices in the footer.

It's your book. Do what you want. Just don't make the headers or footers crowded.

Just remember that complicated combinations will require some serious attention to detail when your book is laid out. If you put chapter titles in your headers, for example, you need to proof read carefully and make sure that they change appropriately on each new chapter.

The third part of your book is the "back matter." This includes end notes (if you're not using footnotes), appendices, bibliography, glossary, and an index. Just as with the front matter, your book probably will not have all of these.

Personally, I like the back matter as an area to put advertising for other books and services. As a non-fiction, self-published author, this is easy to do. It can be a full-page ad, a list of books for sale, or even a plug for your consulting services.

A Note on Indexing

Before you go to the trouble of indexing your book, you should consider whether it will add to the value of the book. Indexing takes some effort. Even if you do it yourself, it is more complicated than just running a software program against your text.

Generally, indexing starts with a list of every word in your book. Then you remove the most common words (a, if, the, and, but, with, etc.). You'll need to remove thousands of these, so you can see why software helps.

But software doesn't know when two different phrases refer to the same topic, or which technical jargon is important. So you, as the subject matter expert, need to cull through this list, combining some keywords and deleting others. Eventually you'll come up with a list of the words you really want to index.

At this point you need to format the whole book (up to the index pages) exactly as it will appear in print. You'll create a PDF file as if for publication. Now you can run your software against the PDF, read in the word list, and go get some coffee as it chugs away.

The software will need to find every occurrence of every word on your list and create a final list of words with their associated page numbers. The output is a first draft of your index.

I say first draft because you need to read through your index and make sure it makes sense. If you have only one instance of a specific word, do you want to keep it in the index?

Note that, once you create the index, you cannot make any changes to your book that would repaginate the book. If you do that, all the page numbers in your index will be wrong.

Also note that a revised, updated, second edition will also need to be indexed. So creating a first edition with an index pretty much obligates you to indexing future editions.

In the end, you need to look at your table of contents and your specific subject matter to determine whether you need an index. Not all books need to be indexed. As with every other layout decision, if it adds value to the book, then do it. If it doesn't add value, don't worry about it.

Chapter 17 – Copy Editing

The second **monstrous mistake** made by amateurs and first-time self-publishers is to skip the copy editing process or try to do it themselves. For people who read a lot, reading a book filled with mistakes is painful.

Copy editing is a profession. Copy is the written text of your publication. A copy editor reviews the entire document to make sure all of the formatting and writing is correct and works to your greatest advantage. Copy editing is normally done immediately before proofreading and copy editors are often the proof readers as well.

Please note: I started by saying that copy editing is a profession. If you are not in this profession, please hire a professional copy editor to review you book. This is extremely important and may make or break the success of your book.

What does a copy editor do, exactly? Well, she reads the book *as a professional* to make sure that all the written language is used correctly and that the overall structure of the words is successful in getting your message across.

She does not write your book for you or change your intended message in any way. She will recommend changes make your message clearer or stronger.

As with layout, the copy (written words) of your book should work to fulfill your goals without drawing attention to itself. So, for example, a copy editor will point out long, complicated sentences which, although they are brilliant and enlightening, are, nonetheless, overly complicated and stand out by drawing attention to themselves and away from your primary message, which should, at all times, be the most important part of your book, never allowing other factors, such as your own awkward writing, to get in the way. Obviously.

In addition to finding and eliminating awkward writing, the copy editor will also look at the book from a higher level to make sure the overall structure makes sense and is consistent. For example, if you say "A, B, and C" in your introduction, then you should use "A, B, and C" throughout the book. You should not sometimes use "B, A, and C" or "C, B, and A."

The process of enforcing consistency is particularly important if you write chapters out of sequence. And, in the world of non-fiction, you are very likely to write chapters out of sequence.

Traditionally, a copy editor's job consists of **The Five C's:**

Make the copy . . .

    Clear

    Correct

    Concise

    Complete

    Consistent

In addition to correcting the writing (grammar, punctuation, spelling, etc.), the copy editor makes sure that you use the appropriate level of jargon. Every field has its own jargon. If you're writing a book for the general public you'll use a low level of jargon and define things very simply. If you're writing for an audience within a specific field, you can use a much more complicated level of jargon.

Finally, the copy editor will make sure that all tables, illustrations, and other "elements" in your book have appropriate and consistent titles and captions. She will make sure that headers, footers, section headings, chapter titles, and other elements of your book are consistent and always work to advance the look, feel, and message of your book.

A Copy Editor Is Not a Ghost Writer

One more than one occasion I have come across authors who have turned out to be very poor writers. They have an idea, and they try to write it, but their writing stinks. They're nice, smart people. But they're nice, smart people who *can't write*.

So a copy editor sometimes takes on a project and knows within a few pages that it's going to be a disaster. They make so many corrections that they feel like they're actually re-writing or co-authoring the book.

Sometimes these first-time authors are so eager to get their work published that they pressure the copy editor to take on this co-author role. But, of course, they are proud of "their" work, so it never occurs to them that the copy editor should be given any credit.

This is very unfair to the copy editor. First, they're not getting credit for the work they're doing beyond copy editing. And, second, they're being asked to do something that's *not their job*.

If you find yourself in this situation, you should step back and take a different approach. You hired a copy editor because you needed (we all need) professional assistance with the copy editing function. In the same vein, if you need a professional co-author or ghost writer, you should hire one!

Many copy editors make excellent ghost writers. Some people actually do both kinds of work. But don't force your copy editor into becoming your co-author or ghost writer if that's not what she does.

Hire professionals to do the things they do best.

This is actually true to the last chapter (Layout) and the next chapter (Cover Design) as well. You wouldn't let the graphic artist morph into a ghost writer, so don't let the copy editor do it either.

Luckily, there are lots of people who are professional copy editors. So they are reasonably priced and easy to work with. You can find them on the Internet or from listings in the back of writers' magazines. And don't forget to ask at your local writers' group!

Note: For a handy little tool that can help you learn to be a better writer, check out the *Sentence Aerobics Editing Software* by Linda Vandervold. It will slap you in the face and improve writing. But you still need a copy editor to review your book at a higher level.

Chapter 18 – Cover Design

Third and **monstrous mistake** made by amateurs and first-time self-publishers is to design their own covers. As you'll see, the cover of your book is probably the most important marketing tool you have.

Unless you're a graphic artist, please don't make your own cover design. Even if you are a graphic artist, you need to go to school on designing book covers before you jump in.

Books seem so simple because most of the books you've seen have professional designs, and the design doesn't get in the way. It doesn't stand out. It doesn't draw attention to itself.

When you look at most of the self-published books out there, you'll notice right away that some look so horrible that you wonder whether the author actually saw the book before releasing it into the wild.

In a perfect world, your book will have its own aisle at the bookstore. Meanwhile, back in reality, it's more likely that your book will have *at most* one copy on a shelf with a whole bunch of books on the same topic. In that environment, the spine needs to be clear and readable. It should be free of cluttery graphics and it should have a font that's easy to read.

Once the book is pulled from the shelf, then the front cover needs to be appealing. The most likely place that your book will be sold is at the back of a room after you make a presentation – or maybe on the Internet. In either of those two cases, the front cover needs to be appealing enough that someone will open the book.

You might wander to the bookstore and look at your competition. Figure out where your book would be shelved. What's to the left and right? Since you're obviously in the business, which of these books do you already own? Which are you tempted to buy right now?

Forget all the theories from your friends who are not trying to make money printing books. If you have already spent money on a book, that's a very strong argument for that cover design. If you are tempted to spend money on a book, that's another good argument for a cover design.

Do you see my point here? This may not be a rational decision. You should take these cover designs to your designer and tell them that these covers "work" in your profession. Sometimes the most basic designs are the best.

The front cover should be clear, should appeal to your audience, and should not be too cluttered. KISS: Keep it Simple! Personally, I'm not a fan of dark covers with reverse type (e.g., white letters on black background). But I'm not likely to buy your book. That's why I said it needs to be appealing to *your audience*. Don't take your mother's or husband's advice here unless they're in your profession.

Cookbooks look different from business books. That's because they're designed to appeal to different people.

Now, whether your book got plucked off a shelf or off a table, the most likely scenario is to spend a few seconds looking at the front cover. Maybe one second. Then the interested party either flips through the book or flips it over and reads the back cover.

I've heard it argued that the back of your book is the most important marketing you have. If someone spends 30 seconds looking at your back cover, they are seriously considering purchasing your book. That's a lot of pressure to put on one little piece of paper, especially since a good chunk of it is dedicated to boring stuff like your ISBN code and company name.

Again, go to your book shelf or book store. Look at the most successful books among your competition. Look at the most appealing books in your field. Why does each back cover "work" to keep your attention? Is it the font? The layout? A picture?

As a general rule, you have room for two or three juicy paragraphs on the back of your book. If you choose to use one of these for an "about the author" blurb, it better be because you think that will actually sell the book. Are you a noted expert? Is this your tenth book? Have you been in the business 20 years? Do you have a unique approach?

This is a business decision. If you've got 200 words, you better choose them carefully. Review them carefully. Get feedback from prospective buyers.

My guess is that your review of book covers that work in your industry will reveal that super-fancy, cluttered, graphic-intensive cover designs are probably not well presented. Basic, clear, designs that work to sell the book will be the majority.

Again, it's your book and you can do whatever you want. But on the cover design, I think you need to really focus on making this a business decision and not an opportunity to "express yourself."

Interview: Dan Poynter, *The Self-Publishing Manual, How to Write, Print & Sell Your Own Book*

Q: How have you used speaking engagements to promote your books? What advice can you offer to new authors/publishers?

A: *Speaking engagements are a chance to be seen and build both trust and credibility. Books are sold BOR-Back of the room. Make up order blanks. For examples of order blanks, see www.parapub.com/sites/para/speaking/formsbank.cfm.*

Q: Do you create business plans and marketing plans for your books? Is this really necessary for a first time author?

A: A business plan should be drafted before you write the book. The marketing plan can be drafted as you do research for your book—while you write the book.

Q: I know you believe the book cover is extremely important. Can you give us some tips on that?

A: Part of your marketing plan is to draft your back cover. The worksheet is available at www.parapublishing.com/sites/para/bookdisplay.cfm?id=35&name=Main. *This draft will help you to focus on who you're are writing to and what you plan to give them. Revise the back cover as you write the book.*

Q: What other advice do you have for people who are working to publish their first book?

A: Go to Amazon. See books close to what you have in mind. Read the reviews. See what readers like about the books and what they do not like. Read what they want in a book and what they do not want. Now you know what to put in to your book and what to leave out.

Note: Dan has made available some free information kits at

http://parapub.com/sites/para/resources/infokit.cfm

Dan Poynter started writing and self-publishing in 1969. He has produced more than 125 books and revisions so far, some of which have been translated into Spanish, Japanese, Russian, British-English and German. He is recognized at the ultimate guru on self-publishing and has updated his materials for the digital age.

His web site, www.parapublishing.com, is a tremendous resource and a great example of what you can do to promote your digital content online. His book The Self-Publishing Manual, How to Write, Print & Sell Your Own Book is a must-read for authors and publishers.

Chapter 19 – Cover Template and Production Variables

The last three chapters have been on the less technical, outsourcing side of book production. This chapter and the next cover some basic technical details of producing your book.

As with many "construction" projects, you construct a book in stages. When you start out, you really don't know how big it will be, how many pages it will be, or even what size paper you'll print it on.

The cover template is file you can use to begin creating your book cover. It divides the file into the three sections we discussed in the previous chapter: Front, Spine, and Back. You load this file into whatever program you are using to create your cover. Ask your cover designer what tool he is using.

For example, the most common program for creating cover designs is probably InDesign by Adobe. So you'll need an InDesign template. But if you're using a different program, you'll need a different file type.

The cover design template is built in stages. First, you have to decide on the dimensions of your book. I have several books that are in the neighborhood of letter size paper (8.5" x 11"). But I have also published a number of books in 6" x

9" format, a very common one in my industry. This book is 5.5" x 8.5".

Once you have the obvious two dimensions, you can have your graphics designer start working on the book cover design – both front and back. Eventually, you're going to have to figure out a very important piece of information that most non-publishers never think about: The width of the spine. You see, the width of the spine is determined by the number of pages in your book. But that's not all!

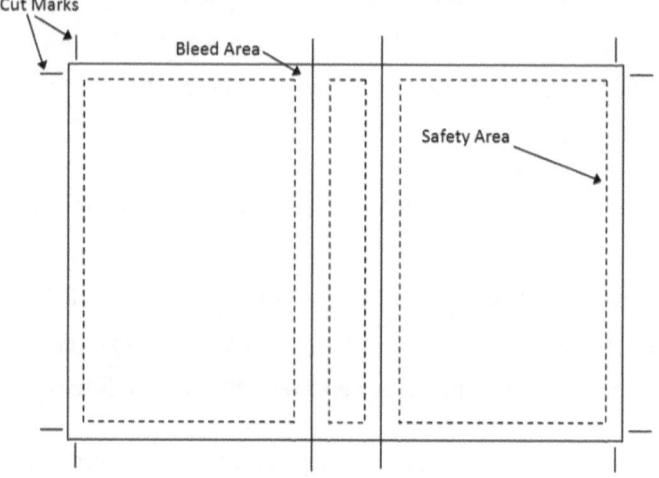

Sample Cover Template

Eventually, you need to create a document that takes all of these things into consideration:

- Front Cover Size
- Spine Size

- Back Cover Size
- Bleeds all around

As you can see from the Sample Cover Template, you're going to print an image on a piece of paper. Slightly smaller than that size is the cut size or trim size. This allows you to have images that go all the way to the edge of the final edge.

Inside of the trim lines is a safe printing area. Because printing is not absolutely precise, you need to leave this "bleed" space between the safe printing area and the edge of the final trim sheet. In this manner, you know you can safely go to the edge of the safety area.

Once you have the page size determined, and you've got a fair amount of the book written, you can begin to estimate the exact page count. But you cannot create your final cover design until the exact page count is determined. This is because you want to make sure the book title and anything else on the spine, such as a logo, is positioned correctly.

Amateurs often have no idea how to do this stuff, so their books have nothing on the spine. Or, even worse, the title is half-way off the spine. Yikes.

Here's an outline for a safe process for getting your cover template created. I am using the Cover Generator from Lightning Source as an example. This is only one possible printer, and you cannot use their template anywhere else. Each printer will have a template generation process. So just use this as an example. Lightning Source can be found at https://www.lightningsource.com/covergenerator.aspx.

1. Decide on your finished book size (see Book Sizes, below)
2. Decide on the paper type (see Paper Types, below)
3. Generate a template with a "wild guess" of the number of pages you'll have
4. Give this preliminary template to your cover designer so he can start building the design. A "real" cover designer will understand that the spine size will change.
5. Once you have an exact count of pages, generate the final cover template for your designer

Production Variables

I'm mostly a technical writer, so you might think I'm so picky about this because I'm a nerd. Okay, that's true. But it's also true that you need to make sure you follow a process like this or your cover – your greatest marketing tool for your book – will look amateurish.

This might seem like an odd place to put this, but your cover depends a lot on the size of the book and the paper you use. By size of book I mean the final "cut" size top-to-bottom and left-to-right.

Each printer, whether digital or offset, will have a limited number of standard choices for book size. Similarly, they will have some standard paper options, not all of which are available in all book sizes. So once it's time to start thinking about the actual production and printing, you need to look at four key variables, which drive some other decisions.

One: Binding

Most of the "paperback" books that you think of are called *Perfect Bound*. This is probably what you thought you'd do before you knew there were other options. Of course you can also create a book that's *Hardcover* or *Case Laminate*. If you choose hardcover, you may also choose to print paper dust covers for your book. Depending on your printer, you might be able to print a book that is *Cloth Bound* or *Stitched*.

Because each of these uses a different production process, the paper types and cut sizes will be different for each binding type.

Two: Print the Book in Color or Black & White?

Unless you have a reason to do so, you will probably just print your book with black on white. If you have a cookbook or a photo book, then color is the obvious way to go. You may also simply have a book concept that requires a lot of color.

Color printing costs more, even with a digital press. And color has other requirements that affect whether the printer will be able to produce books of specific sizes in color. As a general rule, digitally printed books are either all color or all black and white on the inside. You need to go outside the template process to have a book that is mostly black and white with a few inserted color pages in the middle.

Three: Book Size

There are many, many size options for books. And, truth be told, there are no limits on this. But I highly recommend that you choose one of the standard options because there's less chance for errors all around. The printer is set up to pump out lots of books using their template process. If you choose something else, then the cost goes way up, and the possibility of errors goes up as well.

Here are some very common book sizes:

5 x 8	7 x 10
5.25 x 8	8 x 10
5.5 x 8.5	8.25 x 11
6 x 9	8.268 x 11.693 (A4)
7.50 x 9.25	8.5 x 11

(A4 is the standard letter size in Europe)

This is not a complete list, and not even a complete list of trim sizes available from Lightning Source. Again, every digital printer is different, so you'll need to check with yours.

For a complete list of the combinations of binding, color/B&W, trim size, and paper choice from Lightning Source, see http://www.lightningsource.com/client_education.aspx

Four: Paper Choice

The two most obvious choices for paper are *white* and *cream*. But your printer might have 100 other options. In addition, you may want the paper coated or glossy. Each of these has a different thickness. To you and me the difference in thickness is very tiny. But when you add that up to 150 or 200 sheets (300 to 400 pages), the differences in thickness add up.

As you can see, all of these variables work together to determine the final size of your book. For printers who only print "custom" books and don't have a mass production template process, you'll need to calculate the book thickness with a formula they give you. And you'll need to generate your own book cover template.

So, you see, once you know the binding type, whether the inside is black and white or color, the final trim size, and the type of paper you're using, you can finally figure out exactly how wide the spine will be.

Then you can generate the template and design your book cover.

Chapter 20 – Uploading PDFs

At some point you will end up with two files: The inside of the book and the book cover. You will upload each of these to your printer. But, obviously, before that point, you will need to make sure everything about your book is perfect and just the way you want it.

This includes:

- First Draft
- Copy Editing
- Author Review
- Layout
- Indexing
- Proofreading
- Cover Design
- Final Layout
- Final Review
- Create PDFs

(Not necessarily in this order.)

When you finally get to the point where you need to create these PDFs, there are a few key points you need pay attention to.

The important thing to keep in mind at this point is that you need to do a few things exactly right in order to succeed. You will do them all. And you will succeed. All the hard work has been done at this point. What remains is a few technical details.

At this point, the road takes a little fork. If your layout person will create the PDFs for you, just have her do that. You may need to have the layout person create the "inside" PDF and have your cover designer create the "outside" PDF. In either case, they'll hand you the finished product and you don't have to read the rest of this chapter.

Alternatively, you may choose to create these PDFs yourself. It's not difficult, but there is a bit of a learning curve. Even if you have your outsourced professionals create the PDFs, it doesn't hurt to know what they need to do to be successful. Looks like you have to read the rest of the chapter anyway.

First, you need a PDF creator. See Chapter Thirteen for a definition of the PDF format. While PDF is an "open" format and many, many programs can create PDF documents, most of these programs are not full-featured. And sometimes, when they write the PDF document, the result does not fit the standard exactly. So the document will look fine on a web site or when you print a small document on your laptop. But a large, complex document like a book will have problems.

The lesson: Use Adobe Acrobat (sometimes called Acrobat writer to distinguish it from the free program Adobe Acrobat Reader). Adobe Acrobat created the standard everyone else emulates. If you use this program, your documents will be consistently correct.

Yes, it costs money. About $150. But believe me on this: If you buy a cheaper program to create the PDFs, you will probably have problems and end up buying the Adobe product anyway. So just bite the bullet and buy the real deal.

Second, you need to embed your fonts and graphics. The printer is not going to keep track of dozens (or hundreds) of files to make sure you graphics and font files are available at the time of printing. So the PDF format allows you to embed these elements inside the one document.

To embed these elements, you simply need to put them altogether in one place and check the right boxes inside Adobe Acrobat when you create the file. If you don't embed the fonts in a PDF file, the local computer that displays it will substitute a close font. That's fine for 1-2 pages, although it might display a little strange. But it can be a disaster in a 300 page book.

Most printers will simply reject your files if the fonts are not embedded or the graphics are low resolution. This is because they *know for a fact* what it takes to make a good looking book. And it might be nice to take your money and put out a crappy looking book, but then you're going to blame them and never refer business.

Costs

Some printers charge to upload files because they begin doing some pre-press work as soon as you upload the files. They also charge this simply because *they can*. Let's be honest about that.

Lightning Source charges about $38 to upload each file, at the time of this writing. So that's about $75 total for the inside plus the outside. The good news is that this is good forever, no matter how many or few books you eventually sell.

When you come out with a revised version, you can change these files for the same price. But you do not have to change both. So, for example, if you file a spelling error on the inside, you can update just that file. Then, after you win an award and slap a new graphic on your cover design, you can update the cover PDF at a later date.

Some printers charge nothing to upload files. I would not choose a printer based on this cost. Choose the right printer and pay a reasonable amount. It costs money to be in the publishing business.

Note: You have just reached a huge milestone. Your book is uploaded and ready to print. Congratulations. Go celebrate.

Then come back tomorrow for more work. ☺

Chapter 21 – Drafts and Review Copies

Sometimes, when you're in the middle of the book process, you have a desire to print up some or all of your book just to hold it in your hands. For example, if you've finished everything except the foreword and the index, it is very motivating to upload your files and print off a few books to show around.

And, again, after the inside is 100% (or let's say 99.99%) complete, you might want to print off some books to hand out to reviewers or to take with you to speaking engagements. You don't even have to have the cover design complete.

Whatever the specific need, please note that the world of digital printing allows you to get a copy of your book at any stage of development.

Also remember that you can send out your PDFs to reviewers. The files aren't normally too large to send by email. And it makes it very easy to keep updating the document and always send out the latest PDF.

Important Safety Tip: Do not send out Word documents or text documents to your reviewers. You should send PDFs that can't be edited. This is a minor point, but you don't want anyone to be able to make changes to a document and pass it off as if you said those things. Again, this is a minor concern, but a good practice.

Review copies are probably the best unexpected advantage of working with a digital printer. You do have to pay to upload the files. So you don't want to do this a lot. But when you're at the point where you're ready to show off your almost-complete work, it's handy to be able to do this.

For review copies, I recommend creating a very plain cover page that simply says

Book Title

Author

Review Copy

Please do not quote from this draft without written permission from the author.

You can make the cover just a one solid color with no title information on the spine. It should not look like a finished book!

If uploading the contents costs you $150 and the cost of getting a book printed is around $8, then you should probably go ahead and print ten or fifteen copies (if you actually have people to hand them out to). There's no point in spending $200 and having three copies of your Review Copy.

Some digital printers don't charge to upload a file, but their format may be different from the printer you've chosen. So, for example, it might be possible to upload your early draft to Lulu and print review copies, even if you intend to print the final version at Lightning Source.

But since the book's trim size may be different, drafts from a printer other than your final printer may not give you a real sense of the look and feel of your final book.

Obviously, you may want to skip the review copy stage if you don't have a need for it. Just take a note that this is available to you.

Interview: Harry Brelsford, publisher, author of *SMB Consulting Best Practices* and 16 other books

Q: What's the most important thing you wish you'd known when you produced your first book?

A: After creating my five-level outline, I wish I'd known on Day One to just start typing on the blank page. Instead of staring at the white "nothing" on the screen in DOC1, I recommend you start typing from an existing book. I'm not suggesting you infringe on someone's copyright but consider the following. My first book in the mid/late-1990s was on Windows NT Server Secrets. At night, when my day job completed, I'd type out my work, running at an hour-per-page pace. The first words were the hardest to get going. I'd open a com-

petitor's book, retype a paragraph and then I'd be off. Later – I'd delete the plagiarized paragraph.

Q: What has your experience been with outsourcing the copy editing and layout functions of book publishing?

A: *My experience has been good. I retained a vanity press service that "does all that" and draws a modest fee to do so. It worked very well. I would never bring that function in-house.*

Q: How many different printers have you used and what made you settle on your current printer?

A: *We have only used Bang Printing out of Minnesota. My vanity press service (above) contracted for that and it has worked very well.*

Harry Brelsford is the CEO of SMB Nation, an organization dedicated to improving technical consulting practices in the small- and medium-size business (SMB) community. See www.smbnation.com. Harry is a long-time SMB channel partner who has served customers and mentored other partners (SMB Nation has over 54,000 tribal members who are SMB technology consultants). He oversees the popular SMB Nation worldwide events including webinars, workshops and multi-day conferences. He holds an MBA (and numerous certifications such as MCSE, MCT, CNE, et al) and is the author of 17-books. He is also the publisher of SMB Nation magazine.

Section V: Printing and Distribution

Chapter 22 – Lightning Source / Ingram Books

I am a big fan of Lightning Source for a number of reasons. First, they are very professional and well established. Second, they are the printing "division" of Ingram Books – The largest book wholesale distributor in the world. Third, their digital print on demand (POD) presses are in both the US and the UK, and will be in Australia by Summer 2011.

Before Lightning Source came along, you (as a publisher) had to have ten books in print in order to get your books in Ingram Books' catalogue. Why does that matter? Well, remember that part about the largest book wholesaler in the world? Once your book is listed at Ingram, any bookstore or online outlet can order your books.

Now that Lightning Source exists, you can get your books in the Ingram Books catalogue much more easily: Just have them printed by Lightning Source. As a result, you could have just one book in your catalog and you'll be able to have it listed in the Ingram catalog. Now any bookstore anywhere can order your book!

Because Lightning Source is a digital printer, each book is an "original." If you only order one book (or a store only orders one book) it is printed and shipped. Now you'll pay a higher rate for one than for one hundred. But it's a sale, right? And Ingram collects the money from the other party, takes out the cost of production, and just sends you a check. That what I call mailbox money!

Discount Rates

Here's a little education on the finances of the book world. When a bookstore buys a book from a wholesale distributor (for example, Ingram Books), they buy it at a discount, normally around 40%. Obviously, they need to do this to make money.

So, for example, a book that retails for $10 would be purchased by a bookstore for $6. That way the bookstore can sell the book on sale for $8 (that's 20% below suggested retail) and still make money. Got it?

You can set the discount you offer at Lightning Source. I highly recommend the standard 40% for two reasons. First, any lower rate will reduce sales. Some stores simply will not buy books that only offer a 35% or 30% discount. They can't make money.

I'd rather have 60% of something than 100% of nothing!

The other reason to go with the standard 40% is because you need to make sure you don't fall into the trap that has snared so many authors and small businesses generally: Being CHEAP. I can't tell you how frustrating it is to talk to cheap authors who insist on *not* investing in their business and never giving discounts. I assure you from experience, 100% of these people are unsuccessful. Their book might be good, but they are too cheap to benefit from it.

Now, having said that, there's no point in throwing away money. One of the most successful stores in the world is Amazon.com.

Amazon is happy to buy books at a 40% discount like anyone else. And you can set up a book to ship direct from Lightning Source to Amazon. But if you don't use Lightning Source and you go straight to Amazon, they take a hefty 55% of your sales price . . . and you have to pay shipping. So now your $10 book nets you $4.50 instead of $6.00. Ouch.

Also, please note that you pay for Lightning Source to ship you books. So if you order 100 books and have them shipped to you, you pay the freight. If you then list the book on Amazon (or anywhere else), you'll pay the freight again to ship to them. Remember: Books are heavy!

Overseas and Direct Ship

Two final notes on Lightning Source. First, they have a printing press in the United Kingdom. So if you are selling books in England or Europe, you can have them printed in the U.K. and shipped from there. This is faster and less expensive than having books shipped from your office in the U.S.

When we have a new book release, we take "pre-orders" of the book. When it's finally ready to ship, we ship all the U.K./Europe books directly from Lightning Source in the U.K.

The other Lightning Source tip involves direct shipments for special projects. We swung a deal with a large company to give away five copies of our book at each of their events. Of course they bought the books from us and then gave them away. In this case, we just had a box of books drop shipped direct from Lightning Source to each event. This was cheaper than shipping to us and having to ship again.

There are many options for digital printing. Most of them have most of the advantages listed here for Lightning Source. To be honest, I haven't compared prices. Lightning Source has extremely good support. And to me, no other option has the advantage of being associated with Ingram Books.

Chapter 23 – Lulu, Amazon, and Other Alternatives

As you saw in the last chapter, I have primarily used Lightning Source as my digital printer. And I prefer to have them send books straight to Amazon or other online stores. But there are *many ways* to be a publisher, and you should know the alternatives.

I have used four different printers for my books. Perhaps the easiest to use for someone who wants to dig into the "do it yourself" side of self-publishing is Lulu.com. They are very self-serve, so be aware that you'll need to educate yourself and fumble around a bit.

As far as I can tell, most of the totally self-service digital printers make their money on shipping. Lulu has great shipping processes and packaging. We've never had a box show up damaged and the books are always in great shape. But the cost of shipping, especially for small books, can be very high.

Having said that, we loaded one book up on Lulu just to get it out there. And it has been there for a couple years now. And it's one of the best sellers on Amazon within its category (it is *the* best seller in its category for the last 27 months as of this writing).

Anyway, that book just sort of works. I go to Lulu and order 100 at a time and have them shipped to our office. Then, when we get an order from Amazon, we ship to them. We also sell these books from our own web sites and at the back of the room. So we need to have them on hand.

We would make a little more money if we moved this book to printing at Lightning Source, but it would be a minor project to make the move, so the current arrangement just works. When I revise that book, the 2nd Edition will just go to Lightning Source like my other books.

The primary advantage for Lulu and other self-service printers is that they have a bookstore of sorts and your book can be listed there automatically. So, if someone wanders in off the Internet and buys your book, Lulu will print one book and ship to them. You get a check. Nice.

You will still need to actively sell your books! You need a web site, a marketing plan, and back of the room sales. No one – even your printer – will be able to sell books if you're not doing the selling.

Amazon will not take direct delivery from most of these digital printers since they have their own printing house (that is, you could use Amazon as your digital printer). So for most printers, such as Lulu, you will need to have the books shipped to your office, and then you'll ship them to Amazon when you get an order.

This means you will need to carry a certain amount of *inventory*. Inventory is bad. Inventory represents your money sitting on a shelf, getting moved around, dusty, and turning old. You want inventory to be as small as possible at all times.

Once you get into a rhythm, you will order about the same number you expect to sell in a month. But that takes time and experience.

I would not recommend having your book printed by Amazon because they are constantly in battles with other printers. Amazon is working hard to be the monopoly. You don't want to get caught in the middle of all that. Plus they take a high price for their services unless you're selling through Amazon.

As a small publisher, you want your book available in as many places and in as many formats as you can. And everyone wants to take over the world. But you should make choices that give you the highest overall success potential over the life of your book.

Don't Forget The ISBN

Remember back in Chapter 12 when I told you to go get your own ISBNs? Take that seriously. Don't let Lulu or any other digital printer talk you into a package that includes their ISBN. Some stores will not sell these books, including Amazon.

But you can print *your* ISBN on a book at Lulu, and Amazon won't care. The key is to think of your printer as simply that: a printer. Not your business partner.

Remember that the printing industry is in the middle of an amazing revolution that has made quality, professional printing available to everyone at a reasonable price. The printers and distributors are all trying to position themselves to get their piece of the expanding pie.

One of the strategies that a printer can take is to provide a huge collection of services in order to build their catalog. The theory is that they will get a huge number of authors in their catalog and then be able to throw their weight around with companies like Amazon.

Again, don't get caught up in all that. Pick a printer because of the printing. Pick a distributor because of distribution. If you get one house that really does a great job of both, great. But remember that this is a changing universe and none of your decisions are reversible.

Interview: Stephanie Chandler, *Booked Up! How to Write, Publish, and Promote a Book to Grow Your Business*

Q: When listing books on Amazon, Lightning Source, and other distributors, how do you determine how much of a discount to set?

A: I set my discounts at 40% across the board. Amazon wants 55%, but that is just unfair. They will still list a book at a 40% discount and what I've found is that they may or may not discount the book. Since my specialty is publishing non-fiction books, readers aren't quite as concerned with pricing so I don't see this as a major concern.

Q: Do you participate in local groups of writers or publishers?

A: I was more active with local writing and publishing groups in the early years when I was dealing with the learning curve. At the time, I found them quite valuable. I'm still a member of several groups, though I'm not as active as I used to be.

Q: Do you make your books available on the Kindle and other e-readers?

A: Absolutely! The ebook market is growing so quickly and the reality is that the market is changing. I don't believe print books will go away completely, but we are changing the way we buy books and read them. All of my books are made available through Amazon Kindle and Smashwords—which distributes books to most of the major outlets. I also encourage my publishing clients to do the same.

I also have a Kindle and I absolutely love it. I'm a hardcore book lover and like a lot of people, I never thought that I would enjoy reading on a digital device. But the fact is that the Kindle is convenient, easy to read, and portable. I used to pack multiple books when traveling and now I save a lot of luggage space by simply carrying my Kindle. I also love the instant gratification of downloading a new title within seconds. There is a reason the ebook market is exploding. Reading books this way makes life easier.

Stephanie Chandler is the author of several books including *Booked Up! How to Write, Publish, and Promote a Book to Grow Your Business, LEAP! 101 Ways to Grow Your Business, From Entrepreneur to Infopreneur: Make Money with Books, eBooks and Information Products*, and *The Author's Guide to Building an Online Platform: Leveraging the Internet to Sell More Books*. Stephanie is also founder and CEO of AuthorityPublishing.com, which specializes in custom publishing for non-fiction books.

Stephanie is a frequent speaker at business events and on the radio. She has been featured in Entrepreneur Magazine, BusinessWeek, Inc.com, Wired magazine, and many other media outlets.

She also maintains a web site called BusinessInfoGuide.com, which is a great directory of resources for entrepreneurs.

Chapter 24 – Kindle and Other "Readers"

There's good news and bad news with regard to electronic books. The good news is that you have many, many options for distributing your works. And each of those is an opportunity to build your personal brand and make money.

The bad news is that there are more than a dozen formats that your book can be distributed in. You need to decide whether it's worth your time and trouble to publish in all these formats.

The biggies right now are the Kindle (by Amazon), the Nook (by Barnes and Noble), the iPad (by Apple), and good old PDF format.

As with everything else, there's a learning curve to creating your book in all these formats. And just because they exist does not mean anyone will buy. But you can't sell something in a format until you put it in that format.

One of the most successful services for putting your book into these formats is SmashWords (www.smashwords.com). SmashWords allows you to create a variety of formats, and provides a store for selling them. The downside is that they are only available through their store.

At least for the Amazon Kindle, you will want to create a Kindle version you can sell with your physical book on Amazon. That way people see the versions.

One of the coolest things that happened to me after I started selling my books on Kindle was during a presentation. I was probably twenty minutes into a speaking gig when a guy in the back interrupted to tell the crowd that my book was also available on Kindle, and he had just downloaded it.

That's great marketing.

The numbers change all the time, but there's no doubt that book "readers" are going to continue to grow in popularity.

Keep the Money In Mind

One of the down sides to the "reader" craze is the downward pressure on prices. People expect to find things at a lower price just because it's electronic. I'm not sure why this is true, but it's definitely true.

I recommend *very highly* that you simply opt out of this trend. If your book is worth $19.95, charge $19.95. Let the book seller (Amazon, etc.) choose to lower the price and take it out of their share.

Your book has exactly as much value as the intersection of what you want and what someone else is willing to pay. I have a book that sells for $249.95. I sell about fifteen of those a month. Could I sell more at a lower price? Sure. But there's a lower limit of what I'm willing to sell that book for (about $200), and I am selling enough to feel good about it.

At the same time, this book has not been uploaded "in the wild" for download somewhere on the Internet. And with an audience of technical consultants, it certainly could be if someone decided to. So why hasn't this book been turned into a free download somewhere? I believe a major factor is the price. The people who buy this book place a value on it high enough that they don't want to give it to someone else for free.

In the meantime, $1.99 downloads are redistributed freely all over the Internet. People don't value things that are too cheap or free.

Having said that, I am a big believer in posting a free chapter as a teaser. Just make sure it has a big advertisement and information about getting on your mailing list, connecting to your blog, ordering off the web site, etc.

The price of free is advertising. Everyone gets that now.

Interestingly, SmashWords stopped letting small publishers offer works for free. So you have to charge something for your "free" chapter. This puts you in a position where the chapter is free on your web site and 99¢ on SmashWords.

Digital Rights Management (DRM)

Digital Rights Management (DRM) refers to the protection of intellectual property (for example copyrights) by electronic means.

For example, if you buy a book through Amazon's Kindle program, you can read it on your phone or on you Kindle. You cannot legally make a copy in PDF format and give a copy to each of your friends.

You might be *able* to crack some codes and distribute the files. But that doesn't make it legal or ethical. DRM attempts to limit the ways in which electronic products are distributed.

The reason that DRM needs to exist is that it is so easy to make illegal copies of books (and other electronic products) today. A small group of people make the intellectual argument that they have a right to everyone else's works without paying for it. But mostly the people violating copyright simply don't understand that they are depriving the author of money.

We've seen this with software and music downloads already. Now the book industry has its turn to figure out how to handle copyright enforcement in the digital age.

This is an issue where you need to spend a little time, but don't be too worried about it. Here's just my opinion. First, as an author you probably come down on the side of protecting your work from free distribution. Second, the big boys (publishing houses, Amazon, Apple, and so forth) are going to develop a standard that protects you as much as it protects themselves. And, Third, this is a lot less of an issue in the non-fiction world than in the world of fiction.

I mentioned my super-expensive book. I also have a very cheap book. It was originally a series of blog posts. Then I gathered up all those blog posts and put them into local order and reposted them on my web site. Then I created the book in PDF format (for sale). Then I created the printed book (for sale). And, finally, I read the book and created an audio book on CD/Audio download.

Recently, we uploaded this book to Kindle and SmashWords. So now we have those formats as well. Again, my audience is technical. So if someone wanted to turn this into a widely-available PDF download, it would be extremely easy to do.

As a result, you can get this book in these formats:

- Free as a web page download
- Free as a series of blog posts
- Book for $19.95
- Audio book for $19.95
- E-Book (PDF) for $19.95
- Amazon Kindle for $1995
- SmashWords (many formats) for $19.95

On several occasions I have also offered this book free as part of a promotion with some large partners. So it is sometimes used to simply building my mailing list.

The result? This book sells like crazy! The price is reasonable. Almost everyone who buys the audio book also buys the PDF or physical book. So the average buyer buys the book more than once! This has been going on for more than two years.

After the initial release and six months of spectacular sales, I now sell about one of these books every single day, 365 days a year. I'm not getting rich on this. My profit after shipping , printing, marketing, and generally managing this product is under $10. But hey. It keeps me in lattes!

The lesson: Free distribution is not going to kill your sales. So you should make some effort at digital rights management, but don't freak out about it.

The next lesson: The more formats you put your book in, the more ways people can buy it.

I buy the argument that I should be able to take a book I "buy" and put it on whatever device makes me happy. To that end, I buy the argument that DRM should have some reasonable limits.

But I don't really understand the extreme position that authors and publishers should have no limits on how buyers can use and redistribute copyrighted material. I assume none of them has ever spent hundreds (or thousands) of hours writing a book.

Chapter 25 – Self-Distribution

Let's go way back to the beginning: Why did you write this book? What's your goal? Is it your life's vision and passion? Do you just want to use it as a calling card for your business? Do you want to break into a new business? Do you want to place yourself as an expert in your field? Or maybe you just want another income stream.

No matter what you answer, you're going to find yourself distributing your book through several channels. The percentage of books distributed through each channel will vary depending on the business you're in and your answer to the question above.

Here are the principle ways you will distribute your book:

- Trunk of your car (I'm not kidding)
- Freebies for charities, events
- Sales at the back of the room
- From your web site
- Sales on other web sites
- Direct from the printer
- Amazon
- Other online bookstores
- SmashWords and other e-book sites

You may also make special arrangements with local bookstores or other web sites. For example, I sell books by a handful of technical consultants on my web site. My arrangement is very simple: I buy their books at the standard 40% discount and sell them at whatever price I think is good. If their books never sell, I'm stuck with them.

So, for these authors, I am a distribution option.

Each of these distribution channels has a different level of personal involvement and profit. Amazon is easily the least profitable. This is especially true for books that I have printed and shipped to me, which I then ship to Amazon. Books are heavy and expensive to ship.

The most profitable option is to sell right off my web site. There's no arguing about price, and I'm guaranteed to be paid before the book ships. Nice. Even with this option, the profit goes up if I then go to my digital printer and have one book shipped direct to the buyer. I have saved by not paying shipping twice.

All the other options are in the middle. For onsite sales (when I sell books after making a speech), I often give a discounted rate. Even then, most people won't buy. So don't show up to a meeting of 50 people with 50 books. Unless there's some other major factor, you'll be lucky to sell five.

Shipping Mechanics

There are many shipping options. You'll want to get accounts with Fed Ex, UPS, and the US Postal Service so you can calculate shipping, pay online, and print labels right from you computer.

You'll learn the tips and tricks of shipping soon enough, but here are a few starter tips.

To start with, you need some supplies. You need boxes, shipping tape, and packing materials. My favorite source for these is Uline (www.uline.com). You could start by getting supplies at the local office supply store, but they're very expensive compared to a shipping supply outfit.

Don't buy a garage full of supplies! The store's not going out of business. At the same time, buy a package of ten or twenty small boxes.

You need two primary box sizes. One is for shipping a single book. If your book fits in a Fed Ex/UPS shipping envelope, then you're in great shape. These are free from the shippers, so that's even better.

The U.S. Post Office has a great deal on flat rate envelopes. The book is delivered First Class for under five dollars total. There's no tracking, but it's rarely a problem and gets all the way across the U.S. in two or three days.

The other option is a box that holds several books. This might be six or ten, depending on how many books you can pack in the box. If you make deals to sell through other web sites or stores, set the "preferred lot size" at the maximum number of books you can fit in this box. This reduces your shipping. If they order your preferred lot size plus one, you have to pay shipping for a second box.

Again, all of these shippers have a number of boxes you can get for free. With the USPS, most boxes are free or have the cost of postage included. With Fed Ex and UPS, the boxes are free, but you need to be sure to match up the service (red, blue, overnight, next day, 3 day, etc.) with the box.

Note for USPS: If your package is over 13 ounces, you cannot simply drop it in a mailbox, even if the postage is correct. You have to take it in and hand it to a postal employee.

Fed Ex and UPS will offer to pick up from your office. This is probably not worth it unless you have a huge order. They charge per package for this, even if they're making deliveries to you every day.

We'll talk about your online store in a bit, but please note this important point: We live in an age of instant gratification. So, you should make available as many options as possible for shipping. We have been shocked that people are willing to pay sometimes $100 to get a book overnight, even if the next day would have saved them $75 and the book itself cost $40. Let people spend money.

As for packing materials, I discourage the use of Styrofoam and "peanuts" – they just make a mess! Plastic bubble wrap and twisted paper are very lightweight and very book friendly. You can buy both at Uline or other shipping supply places.

Unless you have super high volume, shipping once a day is probably just fine. If someone pays for overnight or next day, you'll want to make sure you take care of that right away. We ship previous day orders by noon each day and almost never go out again the same day.

Section VI: Integrating Your Web Site, Mailing List, and Payment Systems

Chapter 26 – First Step: A Mailing List

Pretty much every chapter in this book could be 30-60 pages instead of 4-6 pages. But this chapter could be (and is) the topic for dozens of books.

If your book project is about *sales* and *making money*, then you need to put some serious attention on marketing. And in the 21st Century, marketing begins with a mailing list. That's both physical mailing and emailing. The easiest of these to build is your email list.

I will use the term mailing list to refer to both physical addresses and email addresses. Where a point applies to only one, I'll make that clear.

You can build a mailing list well before your book is written. In fact, most people with mailing lists are not authors. So don't connect the two in your mind. In some ways, it's better for you to be an active participant in the online community before you have something to sell. That way, when you show up with a book, you've got a receptive audience.

There are many, many options for mailing lists. I have lists on both Constant Contact (www.constantcontact.com) and my shopping cart program, Web Marketing Magic (www.webmarketingmagic.com). Both are great at allowing people to "opt in" from web sites, blogs, Facebook, and so forth.

Offer: I have a special publication I produced under the brand Promotion Monkey. It covers the Absolute Basics of promoting yourself and your product in the digital world. Request a FREE copy at **www.promotionmonkey.com**.

So what is a mailing list? It is the list of people who have contacted you in some way related to your book, your self, or your products. Your mailing list should always grow and never shrink. You will use it to make sales and build your online following.

Your mailing list is *extremely important* and you must consider it in everything you do. I don't care if you "live" on Twitter or Facebook: Most people don't. Everyone has email. Everyone has a physical mailing address. Everything else you do is good. But your mailing lists are the most important marketing tools you have.

Building your lists online is pretty easy. You put links to your mailing list on every web site, every blog, etc. It should be very easy to sign up for your newsletter. Make the email portion required and the physical address optional. Lots of people prefer that and it increases the "opt in" rate.

Tie your mailing list to your shopping cart. This is critical. It automatically adds people to your mailing list when they spend money with you. They can opt out, of course. But this is totally standard operating procedure and acceptable. Plus, you *do* get the physical addresses with the checkout process. And just because someone opts out of emailing does not mean they're off the physical mailing list. There is no "opt out" for receiving U.S. Mail.

When you sell your products electronically, you will automatically add people to your mailing list. But what about when your products are sold on Amazon, SmashWords, or off other web sites? And if you're really lucky what if your books sell well in bookstores?

Since none of those people bought the book from you, all you have is a piece of their money. That's good. But if you can get them on your mailing list, they might be worth more money down the road.

There are several ways to get these people on your mailing list. First, you need to ask them to join! Your book should have your contact information, including your email address and blog address. Put it at the beginning and the end of the book. Put it in a full page "ad" at the end of the book. Put it at the bottom of the page.

Second, you need to have online content. More and more you'll see this with smart authors. "You can download the Excel spreadsheet that I use in this book . . . if you go to www.etc. and request it for free." Some authors have additional electronic content for every chapter.

Offer supplemental reports, updates, and bonus content. Offer anything that gets people to go to your web site and, if you can, opt in to your mailing list. If you have a good auto responder, it can make your job a lot easier.

An **auto responder** is a program that automatically sends emails. In this instance, you can have the program add people to your mailing list when they request a free product. You could also set up an auto responder to reply to a request with the product that's being requested. For example, you can tell people to send an email to

report@yourdomain.com

and have the auto responder send the report. In the meantime, the auto responder will also add them to your mailing list.

Many people use auto responders for sending mailing lists as well. This is what I do. So, if you buy the book *Relax Focus Succeed*, I add you to the Relax Focus Succeed® mailing list. And, therefore, you will receive that newsletter.

Once you have something like this set up, you can give out the email "offer" in speeches, on radio interviews, on podcasts, and so forth. You just say the words, "Send an email to *report@yourdomain.com* and you'll receive the special report." You'll be amazed at how well this works when you can casually throw it into a presentation.

Many new authors are worried about being spammers and being generally considered "bad citizens" on the Internet. Don't worry about this. Follow some general rules of common sense. Add people who have received anything from you for free or for money. Do not add every person you meet.

When you collect business cards casually, add them to your physical mailing list but not your email list. They did not receive anything except a handshake. But if you hold a drawing and collect business cards, then they were dishing up the card in full expectation that they might win a raffle. In that instance, I believe you can add them to your email list as well.

Your Mailing List Is a Service

Let me off this perspective on mailing lists: Your mailing list is a service.

Have you ever been cruising the Internet and come across a site that you *loved*? You loved it so much you printed off a bunch of it, bookmarked it, and told your friends about it?

When you find a site like that, you will buy whatever they have for sale. And even if they don't have anything for sale, you sign up for their mailing list so you won't miss a thing. You truly opt in to what the author is delivering. You're hungry for it.

And aren't you disappointed when there's no blog, no mailing list, and no way to get *more* of the goodness of this web site? Of course you are.

When people love your stuff – love your book, love your speech, love your audio products – it is a disservice to not offer more. And, therefore, it is a service to have and promote your mailing list!

The same goes for back of the room sales. If someone loves your seminar but isn't given a chance to buy your book, you have done them a disservice.

So don't be shy or apologetic. Promote your products so that others have the opportunity to enjoy them!

Chapter 27 – Be Ready to Take Money

I know you think you're ready to take money. But you probably aren't. There are at least four layers to the money-taking process:

1. Set up your business
2. Set up merchant services
3. Set up your online store (web site)
4. Integrate your web store and merchant services

1. Set Up Your Business

Setting up your business is normally very easy when you are not in a hurry. Just because you have the structures of a business doesn't mean you're making sales, taking money, or have taxes to pay. So you can set up everything you need before you need it.

We talked a bit in Chapter Eleven about setting up your business as a sole proprietor vs. S-Corp or some other entity. This really is a decision for you and your tax advisor or attorney. For purposes of this discussion, you need to figure out your official business tax identification number, whether that's your personal social security number or a Federal tax ID number.

Everybody involved in the process of helping take money and stick it in your bank is also interested in making sure Uncle Sam gets his share. So they all have to track transactions against a tax ID. Decide on the tax ID you will be using and use it consistently as you set up your bank account, PayPal account, merchant accounts, and so forth.

Under the category of "Set up your business" is to go open a bank account that you will only use for the book business. Do this even if you are a sole proprietor. When it comes time to justify the money spent on your business, your job will be a lot easier if you have run all of your business expenses through one business account.

2. Set Up Your Merchant Services

Traditionally, "merchant services" is the name given to the collection of financial services used by businesses to accept payments via credit cards and ACH (direct transfer). In addition to credit cards, modern merchant services include electronic payments such as PayPal (www.paypal.com).

You should have two business bank accounts. One is your "operations" account. The only services connected to this should be ones that are associated with traditional credit cards. This is because these services are completely under your control.

You should have another account that you can connect to online services such as PayPal and ACH/direct transfer services. These services can put money into your account and take it out. So you want to limit your exposure by keeping only a small amount of money there. Once online sales settle into your merchant account, PayPal sales settle, and ACH payments settle, you should transfer money from the online account to the operations account.

If you have a personal PayPal account, create a new one for your business. You will need a separate email address as well. Make sure that you only connect the PayPal account to the "online" bank account.

As for credit cards, you need to connect a few dots. First, you need an actual merchant service account. There are many ways to do this. I started out with my business bank, but later moved to Merchant Warehouse (merchantwarehouse.com).

You can get connected to merchant services through American Express, almost any bank, or even your membership club such as Costco or Sam's Club. You'll need a business account of course. Check out www.costco.com and www.samsclub.com.

You will probably also need an account with Authorize.net. They are the biggest service that connects merchant service accounts (credit cards) to online services (stores, checkout services, etc.). Among other things, Authorize.net allows you to process credit cards directly when you get a large order, and to set up recurring billing if you have a need for it.

Anyway, set up your merchant services so that you can take money and put it in your bank account. Test the whole process with one dollar transactions against your own credit card. Don't worry. You'll get all but about thirty cents back in your business bank account.

Note: **Please Take Credit Cards**! Time and again I see new authors who don't want to take credit cards because they don't want to pay merchant fees. They don't want to pay for the privilege of taking credit cards. And yet PayPal fees are higher than most credit card services these days.

Do yourself a favor: Don't fight it. Just take credit cards. This is just like Amazon. Yes, it costs money. But I'd rather have 97% of something than 100% of nothing. There are lots of people who won't buy through PayPal. And many only put their business expenses on American Express. So you literally won't make a sale if you don't take these cards.

3. Set Up Your Online Store

We'll cover this in the next chapter, but you need to decide on the software you'll use to actually execute sales. Whether it's integrated into your web site, as we recommend in Chapter Twenty Nine, or a link in a newsletter, you need to make it easy for people to click and buy.

There are virtual assistants and consultants who can help you set up your online store. As with many things, it's not difficult after you've done it a few times. But the first time can be daunting and frustrating. See the links for virtual assistants in the Resources section.

4. Integrate Your Web Store And Merchant Services

You will need to have a web site. You might also have a blog. But you will at least have a web site. And even if you only have one product to sell, you need to make sure you maximize the use of the web tool to make that sale!

You should have at least one page dedicated to your book, and you should have a link to that page in the menu structure so you can get to it from anywhere on your web site. Once visitors get to that page, it should be easy to click a button and *buy*! Don't make people try to figure out how to give you money. Make it easy for them.

Of course, at this point, you've integrated everything so that you *also* have a link to your newsletter. Visitors may want to subscribe now but buy later. And if they do buy now, you will automatically add them to the newsletter mailing list.

Don't worry about making all this perfect right away. Just make it work. You can always fine-tune it. Little things might go wrong here or there. Don't fret. Fix it.

If someone really wants your book, you'll figure out how to take their money. Then go back and tweak your online system so that you don't have to accept payments manually in the future.

Interview: Mark Coker, founder of Smashwords

Q: Obviously, you consider electronic publishing to be very important. Does it matter whether an author chooses to publish in one electronic format versus a variety of formats?

A: *It's important to publish in various ebook formats because this makes your ebook more accessible to more readers. Most ebook reading devices read the .epub format, but Amazon's Kindle uses the .mobi/.prc format. A large percentage of readers read on personal computers, and many of these readers like PDF, although some of them also use RTF, .txt, .epub or .mobi. At Smashwords, we convert to nine formats.*

Q: Some people assume that "ebook versions" are less expensive than printed book versions. Is this necessarily the case?

A: *The cost to write, revise, edit and proof a book is the same, whether you're publishing ebook-only, print-only, or you're doing both. However, it's dramatically cheaper and easier to format and lay out an ebook as opposed to a print book. Ebook formatting is much simpler than print formatting. I describe these differences in the Smashwords Style Guide, which is our ebook formatting bible (free download at Smashwords.com).*

Many self-published author are now forgoing print in favor of an ebook-only publishing strategy. Print feels good in the hand, and looks good in a shelf, but it's also more expensive to design, print and distribute, and more expensive for customers. Although print books still account for the vast majority of book industry sales—over 85% here in the US as of mid-2011—self-published authors find that they can't fully participate in print sales because they're unable to get broad distribution into brick and mortar bookstores.

Q: So how has e-publishing changed the nature of the book business?

Since ebooks are usually priced much lower than print books, the lower price makes them more accessible and desirable to customers, and as a result it's not uncommon for many self-published authors to see their ebooks outsell their print books by a 100:1 margin. Two of our best-selling authors, Brian S. Pratt and Amanda Hocking, report that they're selling over 1,000 ebooks for every print book they sell. Most authors and most publishing industry pundits don't yet fully realize this dynamic.

Up until a few years ago, traditional publishers controlled the printing press and they controlled access to distribution. They were the only game in town for authors who wanted to reach readers. Ebooks have changed the rules. The ebook printing press is now a free service, and Smashwords is a good example of this. Ebook distribution is now fully democratized. We distribute our books to nearly every major ebook retailer.

We've arrived at a point where authors no longer need a traditional publisher to produce, publish, distribute and sell books. The playing field is shifting fast, and it's shifting to the benefit of indie authors. Indie authors have the ability to out-publish and out-compete the large publishers. Witness the growing number of self-published authors who are climbing the New York Times best-seller list with low cost ebooks. Indie ebooks are a game changer, and we've only seen the tip of the iceberg.

Q: Do you have any other advice for first-time publishers?

A: Honor your readers. Just because new self-publishing platforms (such as my own Smashwords) make it fast, free and easy to publish a book, doesn't mean you should run out there and publish today. It's very important that self-published authors borrow what's best about traditional publishers: Don't release your book until it has gone through multiple revisions and edits. Don't release it until it's been proofed. Don't release it until you have a professional-quality ebook cover image. Readers have no tolerance for shoddy books, even if they're low cost or free. If you honor your reader with a great read, and you publish and fully distribute a great ebook, worthy of being read, then readers will discover it.

Mark Coker is the founder of Smashwords, an ebook distributor serving over 20,000 authors and small presses around the world. In three short years after its founding in 2008, Smashwords helped authors and publishers around the world release and distribute over 50,000 ebook titles. Smashwords distributes its ebooks to the Apple iBookstore, Kobo, Sony, Barnes & Noble and the Diesel eBook Store. Smashwords also supplies major mobile app platforms including Aldiko, ScrollMotion and Stanza. Mark is a contributing writer for the Huffington Post (http://www.huffingtonpost.com/mark-coker), where he blogs about e-books and the future of publishing. He also blogs at http://blog.smashwords.com and can be found on Twitter at www.twitter.com/markcoker.

Chapter 28 – Store Software

There are countless options for "Shopping Cart" software. They vary from free to ridiculously expensive. They also vary from single-product versions to something that will run a major department store online. And, finally, they vary from point-and-click to extremely complicated.

Obviously, you're going to start with a handful of products. Oh wait. That's not obvious? It should be by now. You have your book, which is one product. But you should plan on at least one e-book version. And maybe an audio book version. And maybe a workbook to accompany the book.

The bottom line: You have lots of options for a single product, but you should narrow your choices just a bit and get something that will handle at least 5 products. Many shopping cart programs have a low-end version and can be upgraded to more a beefier, full product.

Notice that I didn't say there were free options. You might find some that market themselves as free, but remember that financial transactions cost money. So there are tools you can use for "free" to sell your products, but they have transaction fees.

Just in case you skipped Chapter 27, go check it out. Every single entity that touches your book sale will take a transaction fee. Some of them charge a monthly or annual fee. Some charge a minimal (25 or 30 cents) transaction fee. Some take a percentage of the sales price. All totaled, it can cost anywhere from 25 cents to $1.50 to sell a book.

It is very common for new publishers to start with one set of sales products and move to another. If you can avoid this, fine. But don't worry about the big switch. It's a learning process and you need to find a mix of products that works well for you.

Many people just set up a PayPal.com account and use that. And that's fine, but remember the mailing list we talked about in Chapter 26: Integrating your point of sale system with your mailing list is extremely important!

I am not going to review all the shopping carts out there (I couldn't if I wanted to). But I will tell you about the most important features of the system I use. I have no financial stake in this program.

My preferred shopping cart program is called Web Marketing Magic (www.webmarketingmagic.com). It is a branded version of One Shopping Cart (www.1shoppingcart.com). The most important features of this program are:

- I can create as many products as I like
- Buyers are automatically added to my mailing list

- I can have as many mailing lists as I want
- It is easy to integrate into web pages and emails
- It is easy to connect to my Authorize.net, PayPal, and credit card accounts
- It has sophisticated shipping options
- It easily handles electronic download products (e.g., audio books, e-books)

Now, over and above these basics . . . I manage almost all of my book publishing business through this tool. I have five different newsletters, and I can automatically subscribe people to specific newsletters based on the product they purchased.

It also has a very cool feature to recommend additional products (upsell) at the point of check-out. And I can create as many sales, discount codes, and bundled packages as I want.

For some of my product lines, I have an "affiliate" program that allows people to earn money from me if they put a link on their web site and send people to my store. They can sign themselves up and I just run sales reports and write checks. It turns my customers into my sales people.

The "autoresponder" feature is particularly cool for marketing purposes. I run all my newsletters through the autoresponders.

And autoresponder is a program that sends emails automatically. So, for example, you can create a welcome email when people sign up for your newsletter or buy a product. Then you can have the program send an email 10 days later to recommend some resources out on the Internet. Then, 30 days later, have it recommend your top selling book. And again 30 days after that, have it market your blog. And so forth.

The autoresponder can basically create "drip marketing" that happens day after day, month after month, with no additional work from you. If you also use the same autoresponder for your regular newsletter, the open rate for your emails will increase over time.

As with many technical programs, your shopping cart may have too many features for you to use right away. Don't worry about it. Find an assistant (virtual or otherwise) who is a shopping cart consultant. It will only take a little bit of money to get your shopping cart set up to become a marketing machine as well as a shopping cart.

As of this writing, the Web Marketing Magic shopping cart is available in several different packages. The most expensive one is less than a hundred dollars a month. Yes, it costs money. But it also eliminates the need for a separate marketing tool such as Constant Contact for your mailing lists (www.constantcontact.com).

For information on other shopping carts, just Google "shopping cart software." You'll be amazed. Over 120,000 pages. Even with repeats, that's well over 1,000 separate products.

Whatever you decide on for your shopping cart, make sure you make a point to learn one new feature every month. They are all very powerful and can really contribute to your marketing efforts.

Chapter 29 – Building Your Web Site

Just as you needed a telephone and a fax machine in the 1990's, you need a web site and a blog in the 2010's. And the really good news is that these are cheap and easy to build.

For new authors and publishers, I recommend that you have three main web "sites" to start out with. You need your primary web site, a site for your book, and your blog. These can all be together in one "web site" or domain.

For example, I have **www.relaxfocussucceed.com** as my primary web site. I also have a product page for my book at **www.relaxfocussucceed.com/RFS_The_Book.htm** and my blog at **www.relaxfocussucceed.com/blog**. One stop shopping!

If you need to outsource the actual web site construction, I recommend you do that. It should be good looking enough that people don't land there and think it's totally amateur. At the same time, if it looks too slick it will turn people off. People want authors to be "real" people and not the product of big marketing machines.

Your web site should contain a handful of basics:

- Links to buy your book – **on every page**

- Information about you, your approach to the topic, and a little something to show that you're expert enough to write a book

- Articles you've written, and links to articles that you have somewhere else on the Internet

- A link to subscribe to your newsletter

- Information about contacting you for email, interviews, etc.

- A link to your blog

- Links to social media such as Twitter, Facebook, and LinkedIn

- An offer: Maybe a free download, an audio snippet, a video, a free chapter, etc.

- Information on booking you as a speaker – even if you've never done it

- Testimonials and reviews

- Samples from the book. At a minimum, a table of contents and at least three pages from an early chapter.

Your web site (including your blog) is the most powerful tool you have in your marketing arsenal. It is cheap (Sites vary from free to $30/month.) and works twenty-four hours a day on your behalf. A web site allows visitors to poke around, learn things, and convince themselves to buy your book!

Your book page – the one page that really pushes your book, should be filled with information. Remember, when people link to your site, they will first link to the primary page (e.g., relaxfocussucceed.com). Second, they might link to the book page (e.g., ww.relaxfocussucceed.com/RFS_The_Book.htm) or the blog (e.g., www.relaxfocussucceed.com/blog).

If they hit the main page, you need to direct them to the book page. The blog should direct them to the book page. The book page should **sell the book**! And by sell I mean **SELL**.

People wander the Internet not really thinking very much. So if they wander onto your site, you need to be in full-on sales mode. Ask for the sale. Push the sale. Beg for the sale.

Sell, sell, sell.

To Blog or Not to Blog?

Trick question!

Of course you need to blog. You're an author, right? Your blog can take on any persona you want. You can be all business, half play, totally focused on the book, or whatever you want.

I mix my blogs with personal stories, snippets from the book, examples in real life, news, and whatever I feel like. In my opinion, the more personal the better. But not everyone is comfortable with that. You need to find "your voice."

Search engines love blogs! Blogs change on a regular basis. That makes them "new" and fresh and exciting. If you can get people to respond to your blog posts, then you can start conversations. That leads to more in-bound links, which can funnel people to your primary web site and the book.

Your blog should also sell your book. See the blog at relaxfocussucceed.com – a link and a good size book ad. If people subscribe to your blog, they need to be "nagged" with the fact that you're also an author selling a product. If they like your blog, they should spend a little money on the book.

Many people are worried that they won't have enough to say. Again, you're an author. Writers write. So start giving advice and doling it out to the masses.

One author I know started his blogging by chopping up his book and publishing it two and three paragraphs at a time. Between these posts he writes little (1-5 paragraph) snippets about the industry. All that material is directly related to his book topic and dramatically increased his position on search engines.

We'll talk about SEO – Search Engine Optimization – in Chapter 37. For now just be aware that the best SEO in the world is to have real content that really appeals to the people who want to buy your book. Remember at the beginning when we discussed how a book positions you as an authority in your field? Well, your blog contributes to that. They feed on each other.

I recommend that you set a very realistic schedule for your blogging. Maybe commit to a minimum of one article a week. Eventually, you should try for two a week. You can make them really short. Don't worry about that. There are lots of books on how to blog, what to blog about, how to increase traffic, etc.

Remember: Your blog is a marketing tool for your book. If you want more book sales, blog more. Period.

Additional Web Sites

I encourage you to consider at least one more web site if you can pull it off: Your Name! I have karlpalachuk.com, and it takes visitors to my "Small Biz Thoughts" web site. Whether you put up a site on yourname.com, you should at least attempt to purchase the domain name.

Domain names can be purchased from many sources. I prefer Network Solutions (www.networksolutions.com) because they are big and they have literally been doing this longer than anyone else. They are a little more expensive, but I don't have to worry that my domain will disappear.

Another great source is Go Daddy (www.godaddy.com). Both of these sources – Go Daddy and Network Solutions – also sell web sites and will host your web site, blog, and email. Go Daddy is probably easier to deal with as a total newbie. Just be aware that their tech support is by email and can be very slow at times.

Even if your personalized domain is not available, you might want additional domain names for marketing purposes. This includes variations on your book title. For example, I have Relaxfocus**and**succeed.com point to the Relax Focus Succeed web site.

Chapter 30 – Bundling

Bundling is selling two or more products together for one price. I'm not sure exactly why there's magic in bundling, but there is. Think about those late night commercials. "You get the Ginsu knives, plus the lobster bibs, AND the drool cup for one amazing price. Order now and we'll throw in the lacquer toothpicks absolutely free."

When I first started selling the book *Relax Focus Succeed*, I had very small back of the room sales. Just to try something different, I decided to also sell some books by other authors. Of course I picked books that were on my recommended reading list at www.relaxfocussucceed.com.

Guess what? I didn't sell a lot of these books, but I sold more of my own! My suspicion is that people like to have a choice, and so they choose the guy who just finished talking.

That was a nice discovery.

Then I happened upon another. I was talking to technical consultants, so I offered several books for sale:

- The Network Documentation Workbook
- The SAN Primer for SMB Consultants
- Service Agreements for SMB Consultants

These are all books that I wrote. I sold them separately. But I also sold them in a bundle for a reduced price. This was hugely successful!

Then a friend of mine came out with a book on service agreements. So we made a deal and sold our two "competing" books together for a reduced price. I've been selling that bundle for five years now!

This is one of the great things about the non-fiction market. People see books as tools to improve themselves and their business. So when they're ready to buy, they want to buy as much as they can.

One of my books, *Managed Services in a Month*, sells as an e-book, a printed book, or an audio book. I sell a bundle that includes the e-book and the audio book together. People buy the same book twice – at the same time. It's amazing.

Every now and then I increase the size of my super E-bundle. This is a collection of all the products I can deliver electronically with no shipping or physical product. The transaction fees are in the neighborhood of twenty-five cents for the bundle, the consumer gets downloads immediately, and the money flows into my bank. Looooove it!

What Can You Bundle?

When you first start out, you might not even have your book yet. But you can still bundle it. In the promotion section we'll talk about pre-selling your book before it's released.

You can also bundle consulting services, trainings, webinars, workbooks, classes, audio programs, and anything else you can think of.

If you don't currently resell other products of any kind, you might consider getting a resale permit (laws vary by state). Just Google "reseller permit" and your state. It might also be called wholesale certificate, resale certificate, seller permit, state id, sales id, or any variety of other names.

Whatever it's called in your state, you should get one. It allows you to buy items from wholesale distributors and sell them as a retailer. For example, if you want to buy your books through Ingram Books and make a profit selling them with your own books, you'll need a reseller permit.

There are additional forms to be filled out with the state government, of course, and you will need to learn about sales tax and filing those returns. But once you have the reseller's permit, you can bundle all kinds of things with your books.

I know people who have bundled books with stuffed toys, candy, MP3 players, card sets, and magic tricks. Once you get creative and focus ways to make your book even more fun and interesting, the sky's the limit.

Even on Amazon.com, you can bundle your book. Once you register as a seller and register your book for sale, you'll be able to pick some complimentary books and audio products to bundle with your book.

If you've shopped Amazon, you've seen these bundles. Buy book A plus book B for one low price. Some of those are generated by Amazon's computer system. And some are offered up by authors who know the power of bundling.

Eventually, you'll have a variety of your own products. You may write more books or create spin-off products. You may just have the same book in more than one format. Whatever the case may be, you'll eventually be able to create bundles from your own products.

In the meantime, think about all the other opportunities for bundling that exist in your area of expertise.

Chapter 31 – Your Other Services

Let's take a step back from the book for just a minute. Let's look at the bigger picture of your life and business.

What do you do? What made you expert enough to write this book? Write it down, along with a few other pieces of information:

What I do in this industry: _____

_____

_____

My experience in this industry: _____

_____

_____

The topic of my book: _____

_____

_____

The most important point of the book: _____

_____

_____

Who needs this book? _____

_____

_____

What other topics am I an expert on in this industry?

_____

_____

_____

If you are not already offering your services to your peers, you should consider it. By peers I mean the other people who do what you do in your line of business.

As a technical consultant, my peers are other technical consultants who face the same challenges as I do. I have several books on how to improve processes for small I.T. consultants. This includes documentation, running the business, and even changing the business model to fit the evolving technology.

I started out giving speeches on documentation. How boring is THAT? Well, the first time I presented this topic, I had 120 people in the room. In *my* business, documentation is extremely important, and almost everyone knows that almost no one does it right.

My topics might be excruciatingly boring to you. But to my peers they are a goldmine of information. Not because I'm smarter or more capable than anyone else. But simply because I wrote down my process. I "wrote the book" on network documentation.

From speaking I was able to move into training other consultants. And, eventually, I started doing some consulting to the consultants. As you probably know from buying training and consulting, it can be very expensive. As a seller of training and consulting, it can be very profitable.

I'm not saying you need to do all these things. But consider how your book enhances your career and how your career enhanced your book. You might also have another book inside you waiting to get out!

As you saw in the discussion of bundling in the previous chapter, selling these goods and services together can create a "whole" that's larger than the pieces individually.

Books as Calling Cards

Many people have no intention of making money from their books. They sell their book in the range of $20 so that it is expensive enough to be taken seriously. But they also give away copies to people almost like calling cards.

How cool is that? Instead of a business card, hand someone your book with your email address on the back!

If you are the expert and you sell your consulting for $100/hour or more, then giving away a book that cost you $4 might be a great investment. We'll return to this discussion in Chapter 35.

Just remember that the book might not be the product - especially if YOU are the product!

Section VII: Sales, Marketing, and Promotion

Chapter 32 – Pricing for Non-Fiction

How much is a book worth? Like everything else, that depends on what people are willing to pay.

College textbooks are regularly over $100 each. Unless they're classic novels at less than ten dollar each. If you own a Kindle you can download amazing collections of the greatest books ever written – for free!

My first book was about 100 pages and sold for $89.95. Even though many copies were sold at discounts as lost as $69.95, thousands sold at full price. That book is out of print now, waiting for an update. But the e-book version still sells for $79.95 and sells every month.

How can I charge this much? It's simple: I have a product people want. They use it to improve their businesses. It costs less than one hour of billable labor. So it's worth it.

When I first released this book, I did so at an all-day training at the Microsoft Worldwide Partner Conference. One technician came up to me and asked about the book. He was very eager about it – until he heard the price.

He scrunched up his face and scurried off, afraid it would cost him money just to talk to me. But later I saw him at a break and talked to him about his business. I gave him some advice and a few tips on documenting his client processes so he could make more money.

After the break he came back to my table and bought that book. I made a friend, sold a book, and learned that I need to promote the book by talking about what it can do for the reader, *not* about all my cool forms and features.

Non-Fiction Rules

When it comes to pricing your book, non-fiction rules. Non-fiction books are self-help, technical, and how-to. They are *tools* used to improve a hobby, understand ourselves, and do a job better.

They aren't books. They're tools.

When I wrote my first book, I had created an online forum to gather feedback from technicians all over the world. They'd seen the forms, read the chapters, and given advice on formatting. So when I asked them about price, they had already used the book and its forms.

I used Survey Monkey (www.surveymonkey.com) to ask each person what they would pay for the book. How much is too low? How much is too high? How much is just right?

I was shocked when most of the feedback was in the range of $99 to $149 dollars. This was a 100 page book! I felt bad about charging so much, so I put the price at $89.95. It was still high, but below the consensus value of the book.

Perhaps the biggest mistake made by non-fiction writers is to sell the book too cheaply. A low price means low value. If you have a valuable resource, you need to charge for it. If someone wants a discount, you can give it. But you can never raise the price.

As I write this, I'm told we're coming out of the 2008-2011 recession. During the recession I came out with two books priced in the $20-30 range and got a lot of positive feedback for doing so. But I also noticed that my other books continued to sell at their normal prices.

If you search for "Managed Services" on Amazon.com, my $20 book is right there at the top. It is priced right for the market and the economy. When I revise it, the price will go to $24.95. We'll see if it does just as well.

If you have non-fiction books you need to resist "cheap" pricing as much as possible. If you have a true resource for people in your profession, then you need to charge for it. If you want to give away copies, do so. But the ones you sell should sell for a good price.

I am part of a mastermind group in Sacramento. We get together once a month to bounce business ideas off each other.

One of the jokes in the group is that my advice is always to double the price.

People tend to under-value their own work. Don't do this!

Standard Pricing

To the extent that there is any standard pricing, here's how you can figure out what it is. Go visit a bookstore. Go find the section where your book should be shelved (you should do this anyway during the design phase to get ideas about size, shape, color, etc.).

Pick up the books in that section and look at the prices. I'm in the computer business. Almost nothing I touch is under $50. The "sweet spot" is probably $49.95 to $59.95.

That's MSRP (manufacturer's suggested retail price). Actual prices are frequently 10% cheaper. But in the computer section, the books are normally NOT discounted. So the price is the price.

What do books in your business sell for? Whether you think it's high or not, that's what people are used to paying.

Next, look at books that are your direct competition. If someone picks up another book and your book, will your book be about the same price? If it's within ten dollars, the price won't matter. If it's a lot cheaper or a lot more expensive, then the buyer's brain will take price into consideration. Otherwise, it's not an issue.

Workbooks can frequently be priced in the range of $30-60, depending on your industry. I know plenty of people who sell $40 workbooks to accompany their $30 book!

Discount Pressure

Amazon is the 800 pound, poorly-mannered gorilla in the book business. Unless you follow the advice in Chapter 22, Amazon will require a 55% discount. So they'll pay you $22.50 for your $50 book. Ouch. But then they'll discount it! They might sell your book for $42. That puts pressure on what you can charge on your own web site. Ouch ouch.

Other companies have similar pressures. Some printers price the book for you. In other words, a book of 300 pages sells for $9.95. Period. No discussion. It doesn't matter whether it's fiction or non-fiction. My $89.95 book would have to be sold for $7.95.

So, please be aware of who you work with to sell your books.

Some online stores will accept just about any book if they can set the price, and then pay you based on a percentage of what they decide to sell it for. This might work great for you. Just make sure you know what you're in for.

The bottom line is to be reasonable, but don't be shy about pricing your book on the high end of reasonable.

With Relax Focus Succeed, I was not ready for pricing in the non-technical world. I priced the book at $29.95, and it had very sluggish sales. When I dropped the price to $19.95 – much more in line with similar books – sales took off.

Ask for advice. Be careful about the deals you make.

And to maintain maximum pricing, I believe you should treat the book printing separate from the book distribution. The exception, as with Lightning Source, is when you can get a better deal by having the printer send directly to the sales agency.

When in doubt, start high. You can always bring the price down. But you'll have a tough time raising it.

Onsite Sales / Discounts

When you give speeches, there's a tendency to sell your books at a discount. I try to avoid this until a book is pretty well established. Once it is, then an onsite discount of about 10% is appreciated.

If you can tell people that the book is cheaper right now than they'll find online, you'll make more sales. Again, having a variety of books to choose from (bundling) makes it easier for people to choose your book.

We also create juicy bundles for onsite sales. These include various books, audio CDs, and even e-books on USB drives. The price list has each item listed separately and then the bundles at a super-special price.

Remember: When people are in a mood to buy, they want to buy a lot. Give them that opportunity. Don't disappoint your audience! ☺

Interview: Barry Schoenborn, President of Willow Valley Press, Inc.,

Q: How do you begin figuring out the pricing for your non-fiction books?

A: *We begin by looking at the competition's pricing. If it seems fair, we would start with a similar price. If our development and manufacturing costs are low enough, we might go for a lower price. We also stay conscious of price points where there will be buyer resistance. For example, a price of $19.95 is under $20.00 and that's good. A price of $21.95 is over $20.00, and that's not so good.*

Q: Do you have a few key resources you rely for information about self-publishing?

A: *We are a conventional publisher. However, authors will sometimes ask about self-publishing. First, we caution them* against using subsidy presses. Then, we refer authors to books written by Dan Poynter, John Kremer, Brian Judd, and Stephanie Chandler. We also point out that the Internet has thousands of useful websites.

Q: What has your experience been with outsourcing the copy editing and layout functions of book publishing?

A: *My experience has been consistently good. Conscientious editing is well worth the money. The same is true of attractive interior design and a great cover design.*

Q: Do you create business plans and marketing plans for your books? Is this really necessary for a first time author?

A: *Yes, we create a business plan and a marketing plan every time. It's necessary for any title, especially for a first-time author turned publisher. If a publisher (or author acting as self-publisher) can't estimate income and costs, there can be no understanding of whether a book will be profitable. If the publisher or author doesn't plan marketing, there's no way to be assured of sales.*

Barry Schoenborn is the President of Willow Valley Press, Inc., in Nevada City, California. The company publishes books with lasting value, including memoirs of "Greatest Generation" Americans. See www.willowvalleypress.com.

Willow Valley Press published *Dandelion Through the Crack*, which won the William Saroyan International Prize for Writing.

Barry is a longtime technical writer, with over 30 years' experience. He is the co-author (with Rich Snyder) of *Medical Dosage Calculations For Dummies*, and the co-author (with Bradley Simkins) of *Technical Math For Dummies*.

Chapter 33 – Your Marketing Plan (Revised)

If you haven't read Chapter 6, go do that now. I'll wait. At least review the tick list of things you might do in your marketing.

Now that we've covered all the production and distribution topics, you know that you need a budget. You shouldn't just "do this" and hope for the best. That's a sure way to waste money.

At you take delivery of your books and begin to work out the kinks of your online presence, bookstore, sales process, and distribution, you need to figure out how you're going to draw attention to your book. Which actions will you take to ensure your success?

Realistically, you can only do a few things well. Marketing actions fall into three categories:

1. Automated / Drip marketing

2. Regularly scheduled activities

3. Major campaigns that need to be executed

Automated Marketing

When you can set up an automatic process, then marketing takes care of itself. For example, you can create advertising campaigns on Facebook or Google. You set a budget (say $5 per day) and let it go. Ding ding ding, the money comes out of your account. And, with luck, books get sold.

Automated systems are good because you don't have to think about them much. They're bad because you might forget about them. The worst thing to do is spend $10/day on something that gives zero return.

So even though it's automatic, you need to do some occasional maintenance. That means looking at the ad, tweaking the wording on those that don't work, adjusting your bidding for keywords, etc.

You need to measure the results of everything you do. So even automated campaigns need attention sometime.

Regularly Scheduled Activities

Some things you need to do yourself. For example, you should post up newsletters, blog posts, and check in on your social media sites (Twitter, Facebook, LinkedIn). If you belong to industry forums or blogs, you should check them out and make sure your presence is felt there.

More on that in the next chapter.

I keep a spreadsheet of all the updates, newsletters, and other activities I need to participate in each month. Some things are a minimum of once a month. Some are once a week. A few things are every day.

You need to decide what you can *realistically* do – then do it.

Some of the regularly scheduled activities you should execute include:

- Your Newsletter
- Blogging
- Newsgroups/Forums
- Facebook
- Twitter
- LinkedIn
- Speaking Locally

Some of these (like speaking) require that you constantly search for groups to talk to and schedule yourself. You can't show up at a Kiwanis meeting and be the speaker that day. But if you ask nicely, you'll find that they would probably love to have you.

Major Campaigns

A major campaign is a full frontal assault intended to bring in sales. For example, you might hold a "sale" on your web site, send out post cards, do an email blast, and hold a special podcast or webinar.

A campaign has a budget, a mini business plan, and a specific timeframe. It has a beginning, an end, and goals so you can measure your success.

Over time you'll come up with ideas for campaigns. Any excuse will do. Just look at what the stores do for Groundhog Day! "Yeah, I do need a new sofa. After all, it's Groundhog Day." If they can pull it off, so can you.

Pre-Sales

Perhaps the first campaign you'll run is you pre-sales campaign. This is the sale of your book before it exists. You can take orders for books any time you want . . . even before you've written it.

If you have built up a following online (blog, Facebook, forums, etc.), then you can start to create a buzz for your book. You can set up a sales site and capture transactions. You can even take money.

I would tread lightly on taking money before you have a product to ship. If the release date is solid and you will have the books very soon, then you're probably fine. But it is a fraud to take money and not deliver a product.

As I said before, I'm not a lawyer. Blah blah blah. Just talking common sense here.

So, can you make a sale three days before you actually have the books in hand? I say yes. A month? Um. That's probably not a good idea. BUT if you say that you have a hard, fast delivery date and a money back guarantee, then maybe you can get away with it.

I know a guy who did pre-sales of a book and sold over 100 copies at $99 each . . . then didn't deliver until a year later. He certainly had to make all kinds of apologies and give back some pre-sales money. He's lucky he didn't face criminal action.

A pre-sales campaign is more about the hype than taking money. In the days of digital printing and print on demand, you don't need to come up with $10,000 to get your book printed. So the cash flow is less of an issue than in days gone by.

You should pick a "release date" and work very hard to stick to it. Build the buzz with free chapters, audio downloads, and whatever else you can think of.

More than anything else, *build your mailing list*! These folks will someday buy your book. And the mailing list will guarantee that they don't miss it when it's available.

It is very common to have a pre-release price that's lower than the release price. This gives people a little reward for committing to your book early. The discount doesn't have to be huge. A ten percent discount is great.

Schedule, Schedule, Schedule

I know I'm a nerd. As I mentioned a few pages back, I keep a spreadsheet of all the updates, newsletters, and other activities I need to participate in each month.

I highly recommend that you do the same.

Put the months across the top of the page and all the possible marketing activities down the side. Start plotting out what you're going to do. Include automated processes and when you will take time to tweak them.

Include your regularly scheduled activities such as blog posts. Make sure they get done! And, of course, plan out your big campaigns.

When you look at the whole year, you'll be able to coordinate sales and marketing activities so that blog posts and Facebook updates all point to the big sales campaign.

In addition, if you commit to a post card campaign, you can work backwards and plot out the mailing, prepping the mailing, taking delivery of the post cards, getting set up with the Post Office, sending card designs to be printed, designing the post cards, and coming up with the campaign.

It might take three or four months to get a post card out! That's why you need a schedule. And if you decide to do three post card campaigns a year, you'll need to make sure you can get everything else done.

A good schedule can make all the difference.

Sales Don't Just Happen

As you can see from this chapter, and the whole book, sales don't just happen. Non-authors sometimes believe that anyone with a book is making money on the book. In reality, you have to work hard to coordinate the activities that will result in sales.

If you don't execute, sales stop. Period. So make a plan and execute it!

Chapter 34 – Using Social Media Effectively

"Social Media" are those cool sites where people post up what they're doing, along with fun links, smart-mouth comments, pictures, . . . and business chatter. The most popular sites are Twitter, Facebook, and LinkedIn. But there are literally hundreds of others.

If you are using social media today, I hope these tips will be helpful in using it more effectively. If you aren't yet using social media, I *highly* encourage you to jump in as soon as possible.

As with everything else, I think you should have a plan of attack for using social media. The two most common impressions people have of social media are:

> "I don't care about the egg salad sandwich you had for lunch."

And

> "I'm afraid that I'll get addicted and spent hours a day wasting my time."

Both of these are legitimate comments. No one, in fact, cares what you had for lunch. Unless it's a big plate of ribs smothered with sauce at the biggest BBQ joint in Kansas City. You see, in moderation all things are good.

The social media are delightful combination of what's going on, how we feel, connecting with friends, impressing others, selling our goods, whining about the bad, and praising the good. We all experience these things every day. With social media we can connect and go through them with friends all over the world.

You need a formula.

Different people have different advice. I recommend about 65% inspirational and educational posts, 10% blatant marketing, and 25% horsing around. That's what works for me.

I get followers because I try to be interesting. I post up quotations I like. I give business advice. I say hello to my friends.

As for wasting time, that's a matter of discipline to go along with your formula.

I check into Twitter once per day. For no more than five minutes. Really. I respond to anyone who pinged me or mentioned me. I send out "Friday Follow" recommendations. I thank people for connecting.

Then I move to Facebook. There I check out any messages for me. I make sure my automated posts are going up. I browse through the birthdays and say happy birthday to people I actually know. Then I look through the status updates on the "home" page and make a comment or two.

Fifteen minutes on Facebook.

Very frequently, if I'm not travelling, I'll check out Facebook two or three times throughout the day, normally for no more than five minutes.

I have the Facebook application on my cell phone, so I can take pictures and post them. This is particularly good when I'm travelling. The pictures are more interesting and fun.

LinkedIn is more business-oriented. The good part about that is that people choose to participate knowing that business take place. I check LinkedIn about once a week to make sure that my presence is known.

At the same time, LinkedIn has great "group" you can join to discuss specific topics. You can get email updates when people post to these groups, so you can join in the conversation when appropriate.

Automating Social Media

Some of the "regularly scheduled" marketing activities I mentioned in the previous chapter can be automated to some degree. If you use social media tools such as Social Oomph (www.socialoomph.com), you can schedule your Twitter updates and other activities. Virtually all blogs allow you to schedule blog updates. So you can write four updates and schedule them to go out when you want.

You can also connect various social media tools. I have one of my Twitter accounts also update my Facebook and LinkedIn pages. So if I tweet at least once a day, then I hit all three of these outlets that day.

There's a limit to this, however. You need a mix of scheduled updates and live (real) updates. Otherwise the social media devolves into my robots talking to your robots.

What's the Point?

The title of this chapter is **Using Social Media Effectively**. So what does that mean?

To be effective in social media, you have to realize what it *will* and *will not* do for your book business. It can give you general exposure and name recognition. It cannot give you instant book sales.

In modern marketing, you need to give before you can get. That means that you need to participate in the community. Give advice, answer questions, and become a respected authority based on you participation. Then, when you ask your followers to look at your book, they'll give it a chance.

If you just sign up for Facebook or join a forum and then post your advertising and leave, that's called being a bad citizen (or bad "netizen"). If you want to be taken seriously, you need to build your reputation and engage people online.

That way, when it comes to sales, you're an insider and not a stranger.

Social media can help you build your expert status very quickly. You can use it as a jumping off place for your web site, your blog, your podcasts.

In other words, you're going to build a large spider web of web presence that all brings people to a place where they can buy your book. The effective use of social media contributes to your success by bringing more people into your web, onto your mailing list, and onto your "happy customer" list.

Chapter 35 – Give-Aways and Samples

One of the hardest things for a new author to do is to give away her book. Gulp. For free.

But marketing requires samples. Used strategically, free samples can lead to big sales. Don't throw ten copies of your book on each table in a bar and think you'll get any return. But, send one to each of the biggest bloggers in your business and you will see some very nice benefits.

One of my favorite advisors on business and marketing is Stephanie Chandler. With her most recent book I requested five free copies to send to people I know. She made the bold statement that she will give out as many free copies as she can. Why? Because she gets book reviews, positive ratings on Amazon, and additional sales!

In the technology field, as with almost any field, there are ten to twenty *very* influential people who promote things very freely. The list of people who fall into this category varies over time. But whenever I have a new book, I send copies to these people.

Yes, I lose a sale within my core market. In fact, I lose sales from people who are most likely to buy the book. But I also ask for marketing quotes or reviews.

The best book Seth Godin ever wrote is *The Idea Virus*. In that book he describes how ideas spread like viruses. And he identifies people who are "promiscuous sneezers." In other words, they energetically spread ideas and recommendations, like sneezing in a crowded room.

You want to give your book to as many promiscuous sneezers as you can. Let's say you pick out five bloggers in your core market. One might be very reluctant to endorse products. Don't send him a book.

One blogger might be the kind of person who publishes whatever she can get her hands on. Definitely send her a book! In the middle are three bloggers who sometimes cover new products and sometimes not.

Send books to these three bloggers as well. Just make sure to include a nice cover memo asking for any promotion they think is appropriate. If you get a very positive response, you might actually ask them to blog about it.

If you can get contact information for people at the professional journals in your line of business, send them each a book. A more formal cover letter might be in order. ASK for the book review.

Depending on your topic, you might send copies of your book to radio and television stations. If your book is about any topic for the general public, you will find these outlets very receptive. After all, they have to fill drive-time and fluffy news stories every day, 365 days a year.

Meetings and Speeches

One of the most, most strategic give-aways you can do is to offer up your book as a raffle prize whenever you speak. One person wins the book. How do you pick? Simple: You collect business cards and have a drawing. Or you have them fill out a form.

Once you have contact information, you can add these people to your contact list. That's the price of free. ☺ You will still sell your book in the back of the room, but one free book can be worth a lot of names on a mailing list.

In some cases, you might discover local chapters for a professional organization. Sending free books to these groups is often a great way to market your goods. I recommend sending one for the group leader to keep and one or two to raffle off.

If you can get the leader to also distribute a flyer advertising your book and your mailing list, that would be great. In a perfect world, you can include a discount code so they can go online and order the book for 10% off.

Strategy

Giving away free samples *strategically* can result in increased sales. Go revisit your marketing plan. How can you coordinate blog posts, Facebook updates, a marketing campaign, and free samples?

Don't be shy about giving away free books!

For a little perspective, think only in terms of dollars. You might spend $300/month on Google ads. That's about ten dollars a day. If your book costs five dollars to print, the same investment will put 60 copies of your book out in the wild, generating book reviews and positive feedback.

I mentioned at the beginning of this chapter that it's very hard for new authors to give away their books. But don't think of it has giving away something expensive for free. Think of it as a marketing expense with good returns.

Chapter 36 – When Promotion Becomes Product

Sometimes a book can become a brand. Perhaps the best example of this in recent history is *Harry Potter* by J.K. Rowling. Most of us would be happy with one follow-up book and an audio CD. She's got lots of books, movies, jelly beans, calendars, stuffed toys, and more licensed products than even she can keep track of!

I mentioned spin-off products briefly in Chapters Two and Three, and to some degree throughout this book. Depending on your willingness to try new things, you'll be amazed at what you can spin off.

My favorite spin-off story of all time didn't start with books. It started with raisins. In the 1980's the California Raisin Marketing Board (http://www.calraisins.org) started a campaign with singing Claymation raisins. They started by singing "I Heard It Through the Grapevine" by Marvin Gaye.

This led to singing other songs, releasing music CDs, selling t-shirts, coffee mugs, toy raisin dolls, lunch boxes, posters, and even two television specials.

In 1988, the California raisin growers made more money from their singing "California Raisins" than from actual sales of raisins! (For the full story, see www.answers.com/topic/the-california-raisins.)

The point is: Selling your book might be the point right now, but selling spin-off products should be in the back of your mind. For most non-fiction authors, there are a few "obvious" spin-off products.

The most obvious spin-off products are simply variations of the book. Print format, audio format, e-book format.

Next up are additional audio programs.

Speak whenever you can. Speak to the local chamber of commerce, the Rotary Club, and professional gatherings of any kind. Speak for free. Get paid if you can. But speak.

And record your speeches. Record everything. Even if there's a slide deck that can't be seen on the audio recording, record the speech. In addition to helping you improve your speaking ability, recording may someday result in a new product: the recorded seminar to accompany your book.

You might give away short recordings for free to get people on you mailing list. You might edit longer recordings and release an audio CD or MP3 download.

When I first started speaking to promote my Network Documentation Workbook, I recorded a seminar on documentation. I sell it for $9.95 – and after five years it still sells one or two copies every month.

I have other seminars I've recorded that sell for $99 for a set of audio CDs. These are on specific topics and can be combined into bundles.

In the modern world of marketing, you might find yourself doing podcasts, webinars, seminars, and speeches to promote your book. Record it all and you might just find that the promotion has become a new product!

Interview: Erick Simpson, *The Guide to a Successful Managed Services Practice*

Q: When it comes to promotion, what's the one thing you wish you'd known when you produced your first book?

A: To require registration for each publication in exchange for access to a suite of on-demand Webcasts, forms, tools and collateral by the reader. We quickly realized the opportunity we were missing by including a physical CD ROM in each of our publications that contained all of this valuable additional information, and switched to an online registration and download process. This saved us on publication costs by eliminating the CD ROM and provided us with a continually growing marketing list, which is more valuable to us today than the margin we make on physical book purchases.

Another thing is Print On Demand Services. What a concept – not having to invest in or handle inventory, shipping and order/payment processing! For a new author or publisher, the ability to minimize production costs and maximize cash flow early on is a critical factor in controlling costs while building a steady publishing revenue stream. Even though individual book publication costs can be reduced by printing in bulk, the investment to carry that inventory until it sells has been known to become an albatross around more than one fledgling author's neck … cash flow is king when launching a publishing project.

Q: How do you begin figuring out the pricing for your non-fiction books?

A: Since our books fit a small niche market shared with a very small pool of other publishers/authors, we decided to double the retail price of other books in this niche to differentiate ourselves, draw attention to our content and promote a premium image, then increased the price of each of our follow-on books by an additional 50% to maintain this distinction and perception of value. Of course, this strategy would have ill served us if our publications did not deliver on that value promise.

The more value that an author/publisher can add to their books in terms of downloads like recorded Webcasts, Podcasts, forms, tools, collateral, etc., the greater the market will bear higher pricing. In order to capitalize on the downloads included in the publication, the author should make certain that readers are required to register their book purchase in exchange for the additional collateral – this 'second bite from the apple' provides a potentially much greater value over time to the author over time, as they can now create and deliver effective marketing and messaging campaigns to solicit additional purchases and service sales from their readership.

Q: How have you been able to use your book for acquiring new business?

A: We have now adopted the 'Freemium' model to drive membership to our online community at www.mspu.us. This means that we give away electronic versions of all of our books and their associated downloads in exchange for our members' contact information. This strategy has helped us grow our channel to 35,000+ at the time of this writing." "In addition, our publications have been a key component in establishing our organization as one of the key thought leaders in our industry, facilitating numerous speaking, training and content creation opportunities for industry manufacturers, vendors and distributors and helping us to develop consulting engagements for our service provider clients.

Erick Simpson is the Vice President and CIO of MSP University, Erick is a recognized IT and Managed Services Author, Speaker and Trainer, and contributor to numerous industry publications and events. He is the author of *The Guide to a Successful Managed Services Practice*, one of the first and best books on Managed Services in the I.T. industry. He is also the author of several other books, including *The Best I.T. Sales & Marketing BOOK EVER!*, *The Best I.T. Service Delivery BOOK EVER!*, and *The Best NOC and Service Desk Operations BOOK EVER!*.

MSP University (www.mspu.us) is the largest online business improvement organization for I.T. and managed I.T. services and solution providers worldwide. Erick's prior experience includes overseeing the design, development and implementation of Enterprise-level Help Desks and Call Centers for Fortune 1000 organizations. His blog is at http://blog.mspu.us.

Chapter 37 – Gimmicks, Gotchas, and Schemes to Avoid

It actually makes me sad to have to include this chapter. But I have seen one author after another get ripped off by an endless series of promotional programs that just don't work. Most of them simply can't work once you understand the economics of the book business.

Remember the story I mentioned in Chapter Five: When a U.S. President becomes an ex-President, he writes a book. It is published by a major publishing house, and he goes on the road making speeches. The book sells very well because he's the ex-President of the United States!

Then one day the book tour is over. He steps off the stage. And the book sellers all over the world mark the book down 90% and throw it on the close-out bin. No one can sell that book if the ex-President isn't selling it.

Your book is the same way. No one can sell your book without you out there pushing it every day. When you stop pushing (even to write the next book), book sales slow down, and perhaps even stop.

There are hundreds of programs designed to take money from authors and promise book sales. They include web sites, book tours, "virtual" book tours, tradeshows, post card campaigns, and all kinds of stuff. These programs always seem to cost somewhere between $500 and $2,500, although I've seen them more expensive than that.

At the end of the day, none of them takes your book and puts it in front of a willing customer.

To be fair, there are some legitimate marketing systems out there, but you should be able to recognize them right away: They have long-term customers who come back to them when they've got a new book to promote.

Some of the book marketing systems are simply outdated. In the days when book buyers flocked to big shows and picked books to sell, book fairs were worth investing in. Today, the book buyers are very different – and they all have access to the Internet. So shipping 50 copies of your book off to the London book fair won't do you any good.

Whenever you stumble onto one of these promotional programs, consider how much better off you'd be investing that money in your web site, your shopping cart program, and some Google advertising.

Believe me, $2,500 goes a long ways. If you've got that kind of money sitting around, feel free to get in touch with me at karlp@greatlittlebook.com. I promise we'll find a way to spend it. ☺

You Have To Be Active!

I've had authors come to me to distribute their books. They know I have a web site with a book store. They cater to my market. They see a vast audience of prospects. So they sign up as an author, and we list their books.

But very often, that's the end of it. The author does nothing to contribute to the process. They don't travel on speaking tours. They don't blog, they don't write articles, and they don't promote the site or the book. So, of course, they get no sales.

This is exactly what you'd expect. If you're not selling, the book's not selling!

All of that marketing activity we discussed helps increase the buzz about your book, and about you as an author. But you need to be relentless. You need to commit to a path and execute your marketing plan.

The Worst Modern Scam: SEO

I was involved in creating web sites way back in the dark ages (seventeen years ago) when the web browser first came into existence. Ever since then, web masters have tried to artificially increase their ranking in the search engines.

One trick worked for awhile. Then the search engines figured out what people were doing and changed the way they rank pages. So another trick was introduced. Sure enough, it worked. Until the search engines caught on and re-engineered again.

And so it has gone for seventeen years. It's a game of spy versus spy, not dramatically different from the virus/anti-virus fight that plays out on your computer every day.

SEO – search engine optimization – is a promotional scheme that promises to elevate your web site to a high ranking in the search engines. And this *can* be done in many instances. But it's a never-ending game.

I put SEO in the chapter on Gimmicks, Gotchas, and Schemes to Avoid because I don't believe you'll ever get your money back. With the right tools and a concerted effort, your page ranking can increase. But it can't stay there unless your web site has real content that people really click on all the time.

Here are two examples. Google the term "Relax and Succeed" (with or without quotes) and you will see some hits for my site, **RelaxFocusSucceed.com**. But note that there's also a site called **RelaxAndSucceed.com**. Most of the time when I do this search, my site has two listings above that site, even though the other site is an exact match.

This ranking occurs because my site is filled with articles about relaxation and success. In fact, one could argue, my site is *more* filled with this information than the other site.

The second example has to do with direct hits. Google the phrase "Socrates an unexamined life" or something similar. For years my article *The Unexamined Life is Not Worth Living* (about Socrates) has been on the first page of results. I'm pretty confident you'll see it there, or I wouldn't be writing this in a book.

This ranking occurs because people search on that phrase, click on my article, and then spend time reading it. The search engines count how many times a search result is clicked on, and how long people spend there.

If someone clicks on a page because it had a high ranking, but immediately goes back to the search results and clicks on another page, the first page's ranking will go down because it wasn't a good hit. If people stay and read your web site, then it's a good hit, and your ranking goes up.

The bottom line: You might be able to temporarily increase your ranking, but you won't be able to maintain it unless your web site has *real*, valuable content.

I love blogs because search engines love blogs. I love articles and useful information because search engines love articles and useful information. There's an old saying in the online information business: **Content is King**!

If you want to "search engine optimize" your web site, fill it with articles and useful information. People will come looking for useful information, stumble upon it, and stay. Over time your search engine ranking will increase.

Section VIII: Final Analysis

Chapter 38 – Congratulations

This is a short chapter to take time to say **congratulations** to you. Being an author, with a finished book in hand, is one of the coolest things in the world.

Even after all the years and all the books, nothing compares with the day your first box of books arrives. Even as I write this I am looking forward to the day I get to hold this book in my hands!

Writing a book takes discipline and commitment. Making that book look professional and read well takes a certain dedication to the craft. It takes a team. It takes money.

You may have worked months or years on your first book. It is absolutely worth the effort to do it right, to hire a copy editor, and to have a professional cover design. It is worth producing a professional product so that your book has a chance.

A professional book might not stand out from the crowd and increase sales, but a poor quality presentation will stand out and *reduce sales* for sure! At some level, everything matters. So produce the best book you can.

Throw a Party?

We'll talk about a launch party in the next chapter.

For now, I want you to celebrate putting your book "to bed" as they say in the newspaper business. Go out for dinner, open a bottle of wine, or eat a box of chocolates.

Take note of this moment when you reached a milestone and became a published author. Don't let it pass without acknowledging your work and your commitment. Very few people in the history of the world have done what you have done – seriously. So congratulate yourself.

. . . and then get back to work.

You have promotions to execute!

Chapter 39 – Launch Party?

When I launched Relax Focus Succeed, I threw a big party in New York City. I invited 130 people. We served hors d'oeuvres and drinks.

I spent about $5,000.

And didn't sell a single book.

Now, eventually, I sold thousands of copies of that book. Even now, online, people associate me with the phrase Relax Focus Succeed. If you look on my Facebook profile you'll see occasional references to RFS. So the party wasn't a total waste of money.

But I never had another blow-out like that and don't think I ever will.

A launch party is partly an acknowledgement of your work, as discussed in the previous chapter. It is also an opportunity to sell some books and start promotions that highlight your core message.

Here are the key variables for a successful launch party:

Location. Bookstores often enjoy book launches because they bring in people who are interested in books. What could be better? If you don't choose a bookstore, then you'll have to find another place people are willing to go.

Entertainment. At a minimum, you should read from your book. It doesn't have to be long. It can even be the acknowledgements. You might invite other authors in the field to read something that fits with your theme. You might also have music of some kind. Make it fun.

Food. Will you have food? If nothing else, a nice cake. Many bakeries can take a graphic file and "print" it onto a sheet cake. So design a book cover-based graphic and make sure you get pictures before people start eating.

Book Signing. Ideally, you should have a setup so that you can sell and sign books. Get a table and some helpers. One to help with sales and one to facilitate the book signing and chit chat. They'll need to push people along if the line is long (which I hope it is).

Photograph It. Don't be in charge of pictures at your event. Assign someone with a decent camera to take pictures, get peoples' names, and take lots and lots of pictures.

Newsletter Sign-Up. Make sure that there's a way for people to sign up for your newsletter on the spot. That way you get them in your database whether they buy or not. You can even use sign-up forms for your raffle.

Raffle. Find some things to give away. Not a copy of your book. Not at this event. If there's an appropriate theme, then some theme-related gift is good. Baskets from local stores are good, as are gift certificates of any kind.

Sales. Wow, how could I leave this for last? Depending on the location and store (if it's a bookstore), you might not be able to sell your own books. That's cool as long as the store allows you to sign books that people take to the cash register.

Don't think you'll need 500 or 1,000 books for your book launch. It is rare that you sell more than a dozen or two. I think the most successful I've seen was under 150 copies.

Don't stress out your printer, your assistants, your volunteers, and the bookstore by scheduling the signing on the day the books are supposed to arrive. Things happen. Presses break down. Boxes go astray. Make sure you have the books at the launch.

P.R. Baby

Use this as a public relations event! Create a press release. Distribute it via PRWeb.com or one of the other news release organizations. Make sure you send copies to the local newspaper, radio stations, TV stations, and all the little weekly newspapers in your area.

If you have a local bulletin board service, post the announcement there. Sometimes these services charge a nominal fee. If you have a place to advertise on the local Craigslist (www. Craigslist.org), post something there as well.

And, of course, promote your event on Facebook, Twitter, and other social media sites.

More than anything else, have fun.

Congratulations again.

Interview: Kelli Wilson, *The Clutter Breakthrough*

Q: Why did you hold a book launch party?

A: Writing my first book was definitely an event to be celebrated. I was encouraged by several friends, associates, and my business coach to have a launch party. The intention for me was twofold: to celebrate my accomplishment with my family and friends, and to create some media buzz around my book as a way to build my platform and generate sales.

Q: How did you organize your book launch?

A: As a professional organizer, structuring and planning the event itself was easy since my whole business is built around creating simple solutions for people. Of course the book launch planning and party would be very simple. My local Borders book store was more than happy to give me a small table at the front door for me to sit at for the day. No, thank you. I explained to the store manager that I wanted to have a 'party.' He agreed to host it and seemed uncertain when I suggested I planned on one hundred people.

I was clear I didn't want the evening to be like work for me, so I planned for a local musician friend to play guitar while friends and family mingled. At the designated hour my Dad introduced me. I thanked people for coming, read a few excerpts from my book, and talked a little about my publishing company and its origination being based on my step-mom's impact on my life and her battle with cancer. It was a perfect evening for my celebration.

Q: How did you promote your book launch?

A: I used my social media network and database to promote the event months in advance. I was able to gain segments on a few local news stations by giving organizing tips and ideas and pitching the event at the end of the segment. As the event got closer, I continued to remind people of the event. I had close to 75 people there throughout the evening. It was humbling and amazing.

It was a perfect crescendo to the book writing process and one I highly recommend to anyone who gets published.

Kelli Wilson is a Clutter Breakthrough Expert, speaker and author of *The Clutter Breakthrough – Your Five Step Solution to Freedom From Clutter Forever*. Kelli offers Clutter Breakthrough Coaching in person and by phone to clients across the country. Her workshops and coaching groups bring real life effective solutions to attendees who are looking for their own clutter breakthrough.

Interview: Bob Quinlan, *Earn It: Empower Yourself for Love*

Introduction: My friend Bob Quinlan had a great book launch for his book in 2010. In fact, it was so good that several other local authors have started holding book launch parties, inspired by Bob's success. Most book launch events sell about six books. Six. Over 250 people showed up at Bob's event and he sold over 100 copies of his book. The Borders store manager, where the event was held, said it was the best book launch event he'd ever, seen especially for a first-time, unknown author.

Bob has written up a nice 11-page "white paper" on how he pulled off such a great event. You'll find a link to it on the Resources page at the web site for this book: www.PublishYourFirstBook.com.

Q: Let's focus on a few key elements. First, who should I invite to my book launch?

A: Invite EVERYBODY you know. You never know who might be interested and who might be available at the time and place you've chosen. Don't limit yourself to people that can physically attend the book launch party. With availability via the internet, people that can't physically attend that place at that date can support you emotionally, financially, and logistically via e-mail. You never know who they know might know. A long-distance friend or relative might know an agent, publisher or other industry professional that may be able to help you. In your introductory e-mail ask all recipients to forward your message to others in their address book. Even if most people won't do this, if just one person does, you never know where this viral initiation may lead. If a small percentage of the various groups of people you know show up, these small percentages can add up to a good attendance.

Q: When should I start planning my book launch?

A: *Start as soon as you have a launch date for the book. Any party that is expecting a couple hundred people has to be planned in advance. The planning for my book launch party probably began a year in advance, when forming a rough idea of what I wanted to do and who I wanted to invite. Implementing the actual plans began two months prior to the event. I had to design the place, the entertainment, the food and drinks, the book availability, and more.*

Q: You held your launch party at a bookstore. Is that the best location for everyone?

A: *Depending on the topic of the book, the location of the event can have quite an impact. A book about health might be* best presented at a gym or a doctor's office. A book about playtime for children might be conducted at a playground or day care center. A book about war might be hosted at a Veterans of Foreign Wars (VFW) post. A book about horses or other livestock might take place at a barn or racetrack.

Q: Other than cleaning up, what do you do after the launch event?

A: Follow up! Offer people a reason to stay in touch. Provide them benefits for staying involved with you. This can be done impersonally by Facebook and Twitter. In my case, the cashier was positioned to ask people if they would like to receive a newsletter sharing specific romantic behaviors. This newsletter will be free for at least six months, as it is building into a tool that is worth paying for. I have encouraged people to participate in the website's blog, by holding a romance contest in which people can share ways they have romanced others, have been romanced, or would like to be romanced.

These posts, combined with readings from books, magazines and the internet will be combined to provide readers fresh ideas to share with their partner. The longer you stay in touch, the stronger the relationship will become and the stronger platform or audience you have for future projects so that you don't have to start over with every book. Longer relationships lead to increased sales, more motivation and can lead to future projects.

Bob Quinlan is the author of *Earn It: Empower Yourself for Love*. Nine years of providing psychiatric counseling combined with twenty years of medical sales experience demonstrated many similarities between personal and professional relationships. *Earn It* uniquely uses basic business principles and terminology to provide a common understanding of relationships for women and men.

Chapter 40 – How Would You Do This Again?

Okay, back to reality. Sorry.

When it's all said and done, you need to evaluate whether you'd go through the book publishing process again. There are lots of variables here.

I started this book out with a splash of reality. I hope you've discovered that my advice is accurate and born of experience. Book publishing is a great business, and can be quite profitable. But it can also be difficult and not profitable.

Aside from the big picture of whether you'd do this again, there's the little question of whether you'd do each step the same way. Would you choose this printer again? Would you follow a different path for the cover design? And so forth.

Obviously, I have decided that I can make the book business work for me. At this point I have about a dozen products that sell *something* every month. Some are books. Some are audio CDs, some are paid podcasts, and some are bundles.

As I mentioned in Chapter 36, sometimes the product isn't the book. Sometimes the product is *you*. Sometimes it's consulting. Sometimes it's a webinar. All of your products and spin-offs combine to create your brand.

With luck, you dog-eared lots of pages, highlighted this book, and took lots of notes. I hope you started that journal I recommended in Chapter One. If so, I hope it's filled with notes about what worked well, what didn't work at all, and lots of resources to call on for the future.

When you look at each of the chapter headings and topics in this book, you should be able to think about how you would tackle a new book project.

Would you start marketing earlier? Would you hire the same people to assist you? Would you use the same printer? And so forth.

I encourage you once again to look for local authors and publishers to share your ideas, triumphs, and challenges with. Talking through all of these topics with someone else who is in the business can be very helpful. And while you might not have thought of yourself as a publisher when you started, you are certainly a publisher now!

Thank You

Thank you for buying this book and using as a resource. I hope it has been helpful. If you have feedback for me, please contact me at

        karlp@greatlittlebook.com

Resources

Books

Book Design and Production by Pete Masterson

Booked Up! How to Write, Publish and Promote a Book to Grow Your Business by Stephanie Chandler

From Entrepreneur to Infopreneur: Make Money with books, E-Books and Information Products by Stephanie Chandler

Guerrilla Marketing for Writers by Jay Conrad Levinson, Rick Frishman, Michael Larsen, and David L. Hancock

Grassroots Marketing for Authors and Publishers by Shel Horowitz

How to Get a Literary Agent by Michael Larsen

How to Write a Book Proposal by Michael Larsen

Plug Your Book! Online Book Marketing for Authors, Book Publicity through Social Networking by Steve Weber

Sentence Aerobics Editing Software by Linda Vandervold

The Author's Guide to Building an Online Platform by Stephanie Chandler

The Idea Virus by Seth Godin

The Self-Publishing Manual, How to Write, Print & Sell Your Own Book by Dan Poynter

Miscellaneous

Amazon – www.amazon.com

BusinessInfoGuide – www. BusinessInfoGuide.com. A great directory of resources for entrepreneurs.

California Raisin Marketing Board – www.calraisins.org (Also see www.answers.com/topic/the-california-raisins)

Craigslist – www.craigslist.org

Google – www.Google.com

Information Kits for authors/publishers from Day Poynter: http://parapub.com/sites/para/resources/infokit.cfm

Internal Revenue Service – www.IRS.gov

Quinlan, Bob – Launch Party White Paper – Bob has written up a nice 11-page "white paper" on how he pulled off such a great event. You'll find a link to it on the Resources page at the web site for this book: www.PublishYourFirstBook.com.

Outsourcing

99Designs.com

AssistU – www.assistu.com

Authority Publishing – www.authoritypublishing.com – Full service publisher with an emphasis on new authors.

Elance – www.elance.com

Freelancer – www.freelancer.com

Guru.com – www.guru.com

International Virtual Assistant Association – www.ivaa.org

Rent a Coder – www.rentacoder.com – Find technical developers (ebook formatting, application development for iPad, software development, etc.).

Sharon Broughton Team – www.sharonbroughtonteam.com – The Techie Virtual Assistant.

Shel Horowitz – www.grassrootsmarketingforauthors.com – Book publishing and marketing consultant. Author of eight books. OFFER: Receive a free e-copy of *Grassroots Marketing for Authors and Publishers* with every order for consulting or copywriting.

Umbach Consulting – www.umbachconsulting.com – Editing, book formatting for POD publishing, and related services, including helping clients figure out what they really need or want.

Virtual Author's Assistant – http://yourauthorsassistant.ning.com

Sales and Marketing

Constant Contact – www.constantcontact.com

Costco – www.costco.com – Merchant services

Merchant Warehouse – www.merchantwarehouse.com – Merchant services at a great price

Order form example for back of the room sales (from Dan Poynter): http://parapub.com/sites/para/speaking/formsbank.cfm

PayPal – www.paypal.com

Promotion Monkey – www.promotionmonkey.com (See special offer in Chapter 26)

PR Web – www.PRWeb.com – Press release service

Sam's Club – www.samsclub.com – Merchant services

Web Marketing Magic – www.webmarketingmagic .com – Full-featured shopping cart.

Shipping

Fed Ex – www.fedex.com

Uline – www.uline.com – Shipping supplies

UPS – www.UPS.com

U.S. Postal Service – www.USPS.com

Social Media

Facebook – www.facebook.com

Google Groups – http://groups.google.com

LinkedIn – www.linkedin.com

Meetup – www.Meetup.com

Social Oomph – www.socialoomph.com

Twitter – www.twitter.com

Yahoo Groups – http://groups.yahoo.com

Tools

Adobe – www.Adobe.com – Fonts, Acrobat, InDesign, and other tools

Basecamp – www.basecamphq.com – Online project management.

Bowker – www.Bowker.com – Buy ISBNs, graphics, and related services

Central Desktop – www.centraldesktop.com – Online project management.

Copyright Office (U.S.) – www.copyright.gov.
Also see www.copyright.gov/register/index.html for E-filing of copyrights for e-products.
and see www.copyright.gov/circs/circ1.pdf Regarding the topic of automatic penalties and related protections.

Go Daddy – www.godaddy.com – Domain name registration

Grader – www.grader.com – Excellent site for grading your online presence. Includes Websitegrader, Bloggrader, and more.

Lulu – www.Lulu.com

ISBN.org – www.isbn.org

Library of Congress – www.loc.gov/publish

Library of Congress publication: "How to Investigate the Copyright Status of a Work." This is found here: http://www.copyright.gov/circs/circ22.pdf

Lightning Source – Cover Creator – www.lightningsource.com/covergenerator.aspx

Lightning Source – http://www.lightningsource.com/client_education.aspx

My Identifiers – www.myidentifiers.com – All things ISBN

Network Solutions – www.networksolutions.com – Domain name registration

PDF Index Creator – www.acrobotics.net – This is a serious do-it-yourself tool. If you don't own the real Adobe Acrobat, or you're not technically inclined, you won't like this. See the Outsourcing section.

Sharefile – www.Sharefile.com – My favorite online file sharing service. Great for moving large files.

Smashwords – www.smashwords.com – Great service for putting your book into a variety of e-formats. Also provides a store for selling them.

Smashwords Style Guide –free download at www.Smashwords.com

Survey Monkey – www.surveymonkey.com

TeamworkPM – www.teamworkpm.net – Online project management.

Worksheet – for designing your book cover (from Dan Poynter)

www.parapublishing.com/sites/para/bookdisplay.cfm?id=35&name=Main.

Writers / Publishers

California Writers Club – www.calwriters.org

"East of Eden" writers conference – www.southbaywriters.com

Independent Book Publishers Association (IBPA) – www.pma-online.org

Michael Larsen, literary agent – www.larsenpomada.com. His blog is at www.sfwriters.info/blog.

San Francisco Writers Conference – www.sfwriters.info

The San Francisco Writers University – www.sfwritersu.com

The Small Publishers Association of North America (SPAN) – www.spannet.org

Willow Valley Press, Inc. http://www.willowvalleypress.com

Connect With Me Online

Thank you for investing in this book – and for taking the publishing profession seriously. We all benefit as the quality of self-publication rises. If you want to contact me for any reason, please email me at karlp@greatlittlebook.com.

You can also find me here:

<u>Social Media</u>

- o **Facebook**: www.Facebook.com/karlpalachuk
  Or www.Facebook.com/yourfirstbook
- o **LinkedIn**: www.linkedin.com/in/karlpalachuk
- o **Twitter**: www.twitter.com/karlpalachuk

<u>My Web Sites</u>

- o www.SMBBooks.com
- o www.GreatLittleBook.com
- o www.RelaxFocusSucceed.com
- o www.PromotionMonkey.com

And of course there's a web site with updated Resource information at **www.PublishYourFirstBook.com**.

Responses to *Publish Your First Book*:

"The choices in today's electronic information highway can be overwhelming, especially for an inexperienced, well-intended, rookie. The passion, energy and time necessary to create one's first book can be quite challenging, but Karl's *Publish Your First Book*, provides up-to-date experiences for many to follow. Learn from the successes of others and avoid the mistakes that others experienced before this book was available."
— Bob Quinlan, author Earn It: Empower Yourself for Love

"*Publish Your First Book*, is a refreshing and to-the-point look at the trials and tribulations of self-publishing in the digital age. There are many books on writing and publishing books, but this one is definitely different.

Karl hits the mark on why to write a book, who to write it for, how to organize it, the mechanics of physically putting it together, and the saga that is self-publishing. He does not forget to go into all the great things that can come out of your well marketed book ... including an actual business!

If you are looking for a dose of reality along with terrific information from a multi-book author that knows publishing and distribution inside and out, you found the right book."
— George J Sierchio, author, *Build Your Own Business, Don't Be Your Own Boss*

Responses to *Publish Your First Book*:

"Publishing is changing. The 'future' of publishing started last year. Don't try breaking into print the old way. Follow this handy guide, written from experience."
—Dan Poynter, author of *The Self-Publishing Manual*

"*Publish Your First Book* is outstanding. I especially love the emphasis on the business aspects of self-publishing. You need a marketing plan and financial projections, along with some important business decisions that similar books overlook. If you're serious about publishing profitably, you need this book."
— Stephanie Chandler, author of *From Entrepreneur to Infopreneur: Make Money with Books, eBooks and Information Products*

"A wise and practical reality check to show you how to publish successfully in a publishing world full of landmines, and how to work backward from your goal to achieve success."
— Shel Horowitz, book publishing and marketing consultant and author of eight books including *Grassroots Marketing for Authors and Publishers*

"If you have a book in you and want to realize your dream of being a published author, Karl's book is your complete guide to making it happen. Take it from a guy who has made writing books an art! Karl's guide gives you everything you need to make it happen."
— Kelli Wilson, author *The Clutter Breakthrough*

www.PublishYourFirstBook.com

www.ingramcontent.com/pod-product-compliance
Lightning Source LLC
Chambersburg PA
CBHW031238290426
44109CB00012B/347